How The West Was Won

GUNS OF THE WILD WEST

How The West Was Won
GUNS OF THE WILD WEST

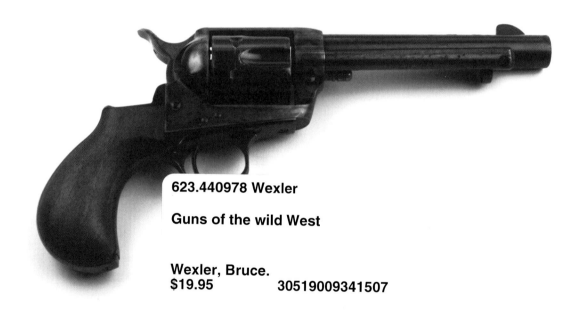

BRUCE WEXLER

Skyhorse Publishing

CONTENTS

"Wild Bill" James Hickok

INTRODUCTION

There have been many excellent books written on the guns of the American West and for the most part they focus on the glamorous end of the market, iconic models in the hands of the slick gunslingers. Our book will look at the fascinating spectrum of the firearms that all helped, in their own way, to contribute to the founding of the West, from the Colt Lightning in the hands of Billy The Kid to the Winchester carbine of the bearded possum trapper and the Colt Storekeeper Model under the counter of the town's general store.

The revolutionary struggle and the resulting Bill of Rights gave American citizens the right to bear arms. The subliminal idea behind this was that Americans would be able to rise up against a despotic government of the kind that they left their original countries to avoid. Firearms freely circulating in the hands of citizens was never encouraged in Europe because of the threat that it posed to the ruling monarchies. Americans had a different agenda. Add to this the skills in handling firearms gained by much of the male population and the meteoric rise in American weapon technology during the Civil War, and you have the potent cocktail that created the "Wild" West. We will also examine the Civil War weaponry that gave birth to many of the guns used on the Western Frontier. Skills gained riding in the cavalry of both sides of the conflict gave birth to a breed of men that made the cattle drives possible. They used their Winchesters and Colts to ward off hungry Indians and predators. Even before the war there were the Mountain Men who began the task of carving out the pathways of Western expansion. There were also the hostilities fought against Mexico for the lands of Texas and the Southwest. These campaigns were all part of driving the Frontier ever westward so that the country would eventually become one, stretching from the Jersey shore to the Pacific coast. Every mile of this territory was hard fought for, using the firearms that make up our book.

Opposite: Wild Bill Hickok who wore his guns backwards for a fast draw.

Above: The second amendment of the United States Constitution.

THE EARLY DAYS

Carving a mighty nation out of a massive Continent is not easy. The British, German, and Scots-Irish settlers that had assembled on the Eastern seaboard of America needed to find a way West to unlock the true potential of their new country. The first challenge was crossing mountain ranges like the mighty Appalachians, beyond which lay the Indian tribes forming a human barrier to Western expansion. The South and West had been colonized by the French and Spanish. Their colonies differed in composition from those of the other European settlers. The aim of Spain and France was the extraction of American resources to send back home rather than looking to settle long-term. Because of this their settlements were quite lightly populated. By the time of the 1763 Treaty of Paris, the British colonists numbered over one and a half million people. They had settled in self-sufficient communities, working the land and utilizing local resources. The British Government soon regarded these American settlers as an important overseas market for its growing industrial output.

But the restrictions that the British government placed on further Western expansion caused bitter resentment in the more adventurous and land-hungry settlers. The colonists were independently minded people who, in many cases, had left Europe to escape the restrictions of established churches and monarch-orientated governments. Understandably, they resented limitations being imposed on their lives in the New World by the corrupt regimes they thought they had left behind. This unwarranted interference led to the seeds of revolution being sown among the settlers.

After the American War of Independence, the constitution of 1787 enshrined the need for expansion. Leaders such as Madison and Jefferson regarded westward expansion as an absolute necessity. The War had also imparted another cornerstone of America's constitution: the right to bear arms. This was to have a significant impact on westward expansion and the founding of the United States of America.

Opposite: As the settlers made their way West, few could have imagined the spectacular scenery they would encounter.

Below: The Charleville musket was supplied in large numbers to the Americans by the French to assist them in their revolutionary struggle. Consequently the gun was widely available.

THE MOUNTAIN MEN

Opposite: American artist William de la Montagne Cary depicts two famous mountain men, Jim Bridger and Scottish aristocrat Sir William Drummond-Stewart.

Americans began to turn their eyes to the West at the end of the eighteenth century, but they couldn't see beyond the impenetrable wall of the Rockies. This barrier eventually came down thanks to a band of men, each of whom was part adventurer, part explorer, part Indian fighter, and part fur-trapper. They risked their lives up there in the high mountains, deep canyons, and broad windswept meadows of the Rocky Mountain terrain. This was a new breed of American called the mountain man.

Between the years 1807 and 1840, when the fur trade dominated in the Rockies, thousands of these men came and went from the region. Each of them made his own personal contribution to the mountain man legend. Only a handful of their individual stories have survived, but each and every one of them was a textbook example of a rugged individualist. The typical mountain trapper was a man in his twenties or thirties from the southern states, the Midwest, or from the farms of Canada. Nearly all of these men had been brought up on farms. Trappers from the urban Northeast were almost nonexistent. Even though the fur companies preferred to hire bachelors, a surprising majority of the fur trappers were married men. But they left their wives behind when they went into the wilderness like soldiers marching off to war. These men were highly dependent on their weapons and needed to choose them carefully so that they could survive the difficult and dangerous conditions they faced in the mountains.

PLAINS RIFLES

The first mountain men used adapted military rifles, many of which had hardly evolved from the War of Independence. A particular favorite was the 1803 Model flintlock rifle, Harpers Ferry Model. Also popular were modified versions of the French Charleville flintlock muskets which were imported en masse from the Charleville-Mezieres armory in the Ardennes region of France during the war of Independence with Britain. These were mostly smooth bore guns designed for quick loading in the heat of battle rather than the accuracy needed for hunting or Indian fighting. Although the percussion system appeared later in the period of westward

expansion, many mountain men stayed with the flintlock system because of its reliability. These guns were also convenient because they didn't require a renewable supply of caps which was a serious consideration when everything had to be hand-carried into the mountains.

HARPERS FERRY MODEL	
CALIBER: .54	
LENGTH OF BARREL: 36 INCHES	
BARREL SHAPE: PART OCTAGONAL	
FINISH: WALNUT STOCK WITH BRASS FITTINGS - RAMROD PIPES, BUTTPLATE, PATCHBOX, AND TRIGGER GUARD	

Above: Harpers Ferry Model 1803
Another example of the 1803 Rifle but with a modified barrel of 32 inches.

Above: Unmarked full-stock flintlock Kentucky rifle with engraving on patchbox.

FLINTLOCK KENTUCKY RIFLE	
CALIBER: .32	
LENGTH OF BARREL: 36 INCHES	
BARREL SHAPE: OCTAGONAL	
FINISH: MAPLE STOCK	

Right: The lock of this Model 1803 bears the mark Harpers Ferry 1819.

Below: A fine example of the Harpers Ferry Model 1803 flintlock rifle with a full-length barrel.

KENTUCKY FLINTLOCK RIFLE	
CALIBER: .41	
LENGTH OF BARREL: 40 INCHES	
BARREL SHAPE: OCTAGONAL	
FINISH: MAPLE WITH BRASS FORE-END CAP	

Below: Kentucky flintlock rifle. The backwoodsmen used the longer and heavier, but smaller-bore Kentucky rifle. Many of these found their way up into the mountains. Ultimately, they lacked the stopping power needed for larger game.

Left: Close-up of the intricate engraving which characterized many mountain men guns and equipment. It is possible that the hardships of their everyday lives needed the counterbalance of some finesse. The scene depicts hunting deer with some flower motifs.

Over time, the mountain men's rifles evolved into more accurate pieces with heavier and shorter barrels that were rifled.

To satisfy the demand for accurate rifles, a number of gunsmiths set up shop in St. Louis, Missouri. The city was known as "the Gateway to the West" and was the starting point for many expeditions that travelled upriver into the mountains. Jacob Hawken and his brother Samuel were two such men. Their name became synonymous with the iconic plains rifles they manufactured. Essentially, the plains rifle was manufactured with a heavy

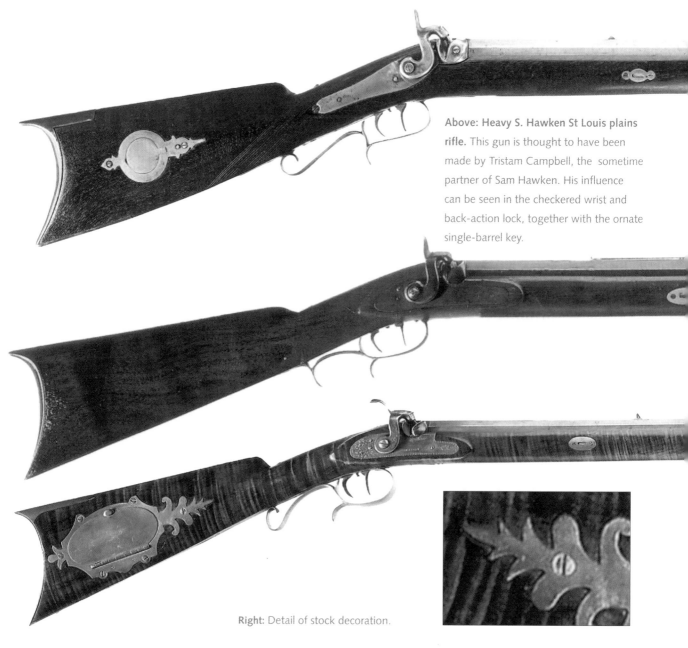

Above: Heavy S. Hawken St Louis plains rifle. This gun is thought to have been made by Tristam Campbell, the sometime partner of Sam Hawken. His influence can be seen in the checkered wrist and back-action lock, together with the ornate single-barrel key.

Right: Detail of stock decoration.

HEAVY S. HAWKEN ST LOUIS PLAINS RIFLE

CALIBER: .45

LENGTH OF BARREL: 33 INCHES

BARREL SHAPE: OCTAGONAL BARREL

FINISH: WALNUT STOCK

but relatively short octagonal barrel. These firearms were all large caliber, usually over .45 caliber. This gave them excellent stopping power for large game such as buffalo or grizzly bear. It was no good hitting either of these large animals with a .36 as this would probably only wound them. The guns were half-stocked and were required to have a high standard of finish. This included ornate patchboxes, scrolled trigger guards, fancy hammers, and engraved lock plates. Apart from his pipe, a mountain man's gun was probably his most treasured possession. Many of them were prepared to spend a bit extra to get a really good firearm.

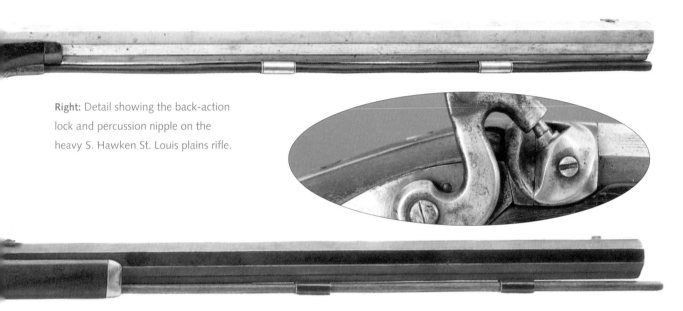

Right: Detail showing the back-action lock and percussion nipple on the heavy S. Hawken St. Louis plains rifle.

Above: Hawken Shop Gemmer percussion half-stock rifle In 1864 J.P. Gemmer bought-out the Hawken business and continued to make guns in the Hawken tradition until 1915. This example is a late plains rifle but it retains all of the classic characteristics. Guns of this type continued to be used for many years on the frontier.

Above: A classic two-pin half-stock percussion rifle. This gun is marked "S.Hawken St. Louis" on the top of the Barrel. It is a fine example of a longer-barreled plains rifle. It is made from high-grade tiger-stripe maple.

ABOVE: Samuel Hawken's maker's mark etched onto the barrel of a St. Louis plains rifle.

HANDGUNS

As with rifles, the main source of handguns available to the mountain man would have been ex-military issue weapons. Expensive European imported pistols were beyond the budget of the average trapper, so he would probably rely on the United States martial models of the day. These would be generally be flintlock weapons and, for practical reasons, the mountain man's preferred mechanism. The trappers carried pistols for personal protection rather than for hunting, as they were quicker to swing into action than heavy plains rifles. A pistol could be worn on the belt and taken into narrow places where a rifle wouldn't fit. This reflected how the pistol was used by the frontier gunslingers.

MODEL 1813 ARMY FLINTLOCK PISTOL	
CALIBER: .69	
LENGTH OF BARREL: 9¹/₁₆ INCHES	
FINISH: WALNUT STOCK, HICKORY RAMROD	

Below: Model 1813 Army flintlock pistol. This was one of the first guns to have interchangeable parts.

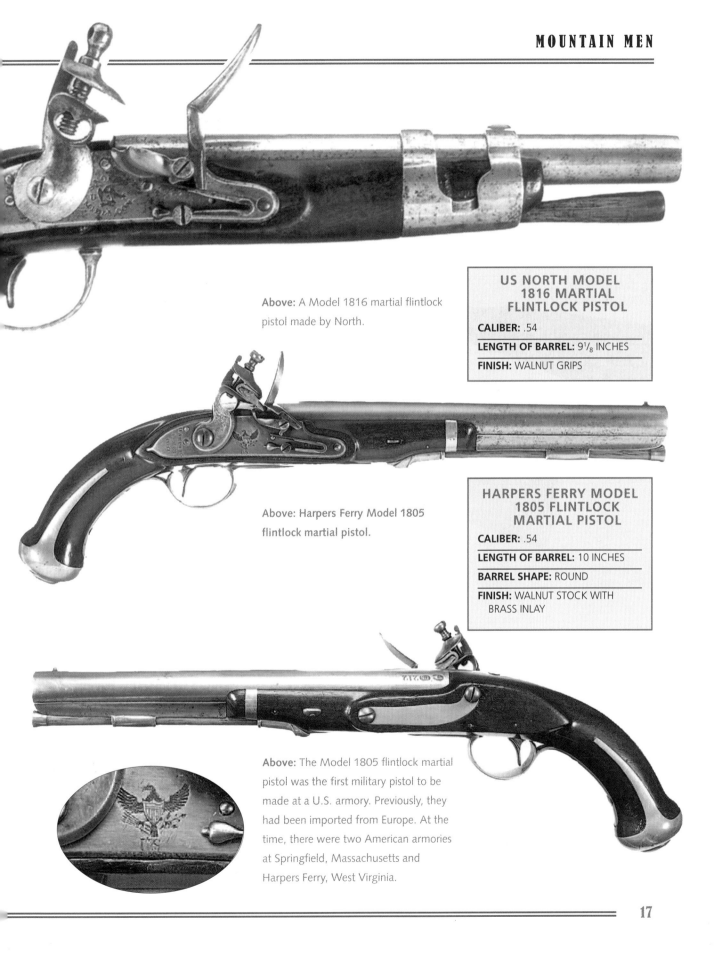

Above: A Model 1816 martial flintlock pistol made by North.

US NORTH MODEL 1816 MARTIAL FLINTLOCK PISTOL

CALIBER: .54

LENGTH OF BARREL: 9 1/8 INCHES

FINISH: WALNUT GRIPS

Above: Harpers Ferry Model 1805 flintlock martial pistol.

HARPERS FERRY MODEL 1805 FLINTLOCK MARTIAL PISTOL

CALIBER: .54

LENGTH OF BARREL: 10 INCHES

BARREL SHAPE: ROUND

FINISH: WALNUT STOCK WITH BRASS INLAY

Above: The Model 1805 flintlock martial pistol was the first military pistol to be made at a U.S. armory. Previously, they had been imported from Europe. At the time, there were two American armories at Springfield, Massachusetts and Harpers Ferry, West Virginia.

TRADE MUSKETS

Trade muskets were the main firearms used by Native Americans in the era of the mountain men. Usually the guns had been traded to them by companies such as the Hudson's Bay Company in return for precious furs. For the most part, these trade muskets were cheaply designed and made and were far inferior guns to those at the disposal of the mountain

Above: Hudson's Bay Indian trade musket by Hollis & Sons, makers to the British royal family.

men and to those used by the British Army. At this time, the British army was stationed just over the border in Canada. In fact, the basic design of the trade muskets was quite deliberate. The guns were made to be deliberately simple and robust as it was thought that Native Americans would be unable to maintain and care for the weapons. This turned out not to be the case, and many well–cared for examples have survived.

Left: The flintlock mechanism of a Barnett Trade Rifle.

Above: Barnett London Indian trade flint musket marked "Barnett London."

BARNETT LONDON INDIAN TRADE FLINT MUSKET	
CALIBER: .62 SMOOTHBORE	
LENGTH OF BARREL: 40 INCHES	
BARREL SHAPE: OCTAGONAL BREECH/ROUND BARREL	
FINISH: WALNUT STOCK	

HUDSON'S BAY INDIAN TRADE MUSKET	
CALIBER: .58	
LENGTH OF BARREL: 36 INCHES	
BARREL SHAPE: ROUND	
FINISH: HARDWOOD	

Below: Early Ketland Northwest Indian trade musket. There is a good example of Indian brass tack decoration on the stock. This is made from dark tiger maple wood. The gun has been converted from flintlock to percussion cap.

EARLY KETLAND NORTHWEST INDIAN TRADE MUSKET.	
CALIBER: .60 SMOOTHBORE	
LENGTH OF BARREL: 35 INCHES	
BARREL SHAPE: OCTAGONAL /ROUND	

Below: H.E. Leman Indian trade rifle, marked "H.E. Leman Lancaster PA." This American gun is of a superior design in that it is rifled. A similar gun was captured from a Sioux warrior following 1876's Battle of the Little Bighorn.

INDIAN TRADE RIFLE	
CALIBER: .50	
LENGTH OF BARREL: 37 INCHES	
BARREL SHAPE: OCTAGONAL	
FINISH: ARTIFICIALLY STRIPED HARDWOOD	

THE STRUGGLE FOR TEXAS

Above: Stephen Austin became known as the "Father of Texas" when he was hired by the Mexican government to recruit settlers for the territory. He also founded the Texas Rangers with a fledgling force of ten men, who were recruited in 1823.

At the beginning of the nineteenth century the territory of Texas was controlled by Mexico. Moses and Stephen Austin (father and son) were hired by the Mexican government to recruit settlers for the new land. But Mexico soon proved to be completely unable or unwilling to protect the new settlers from Indian attack. In 1823, Stephen Austin recruited a fledgling force of ten men "to act as rangers for the common defense." This was a positively revolutionary idea for the time, when western law enforcement was at best patchy and informal.

This original force of "ranging" officers is credited with being the forerunner of the contemporary Texas Rangers. They went on to become both an effective force for law enforcement and one of the most mythological elements in the history of the Old West. They also became a focus of traditional values. They ranged the length and breadth of the new colony, protecting the white settlers from attack by a whole roster of Indian tribes, including the Comanche, Karankawa, Waco, and Tonkawa. When no threat was apparent, the rangers returned to their own land and families.

A corps of professional full-time Rangers was established a few years later. These men were paid $1.25 a day which was to include "pay, rations, clothing, and horse service." In this way, the men were made responsible for providing their own arms, mounts, and equipment. As the ranger had to provide his own weapons, many chose to purchase examples of the newly introduced Colt revolving pistols, from the recently established company.

Before the involvement of the Austins in bringing settlers to Texas, only a tiny number of colonists had made it to Texas by 1821 (an estimate of only 600 or 700 people). But despite attempts by the Mexican government to limit the number of settlers coming into Texas via the United States, an estimated 50,000 Americans settled in the state of Texas between 1823 and 1836. Inevitably, this led to a schism of opposing interests opening up between the new American Texans and the Mexican government. This bad feeling led to the wrongful imprisonment of Stephen F. Austin in Mexico City for over two years. Austin was accused of "inciting revolution" against the Mexican regime, when he tried and failed to negotiate improved rights for American settlers. Not unnaturally, this experience converted Austin (who was to be celebrated as the "Father of Texas") from a moderate man willing to negotiate with Mexico into a fervent believer in the Texas Independence movement. He went on to become a volunteer commander in the Texas Revolution.

When a provisional "rebel" Texan government, known as the Permanent Council, was established by the Consultation of 1835, one of its first acts was to recruit twenty-five professional rangers under the command of Silas M. Parker. Their primary duty was to "range" between Brazos, Texas and Trinity County, Texas. This force grew to consist of three

Below: An early photograph of a group of Texas Rangers. Some of their uniforms appear to have been carried over from the Civil War, when Texans fought on the side of the Confederacy.

companies of fifty-six men. Each company was commanded by a captain supported by first and second lieutenants. A major was in overall charge of the force.

In the heat of the Revolutionary War, men often served as both soldiers and rangers. Some rangers were drafted into cavalry regiments, where they were known as dragoons. The Gonzales Ranging Company of Mounted Volunteers was the only fighting force to answer Colonel Travis's desperate plea for assistance in defending the mission fort of the Alamo in 1836 from the overwhelming force of 5,000 Mexican troops. Rangers died heroically alongside the other defenders, which included famous scout, hunter, and Indian fighter Davy Crockett.

The Battle of the Alamo became a potent symbol of American resistance to foreign domination and was instrumental in Texas joining the Union in 1845. In a further tragedy, several rangers were captured by the Mexican army after the Mexican victory at the Battle of Coleto. The Mexican President Antonio Lopez de Santa Anna ordered that all the survivors should be killed, including the rangers. They were among the 342 people executed Palm Sunday, March 27 1836, in fields just outside Goliad. This massacre, and that of the Alamo, became the focus of Texan revolutionary fervor, and the origin of Sam Houston's famous battle cry "Remember the Alamo, Remember Goliad."

Individual Texas Rangers, such as Jack Hays, Ben McCulloch, Samuel Walker, and William Alexander Anderson "Bigfoot" Wallace, became famous as frontier fighters. As time went on, the rangers also became much better equipped. In 1839, the Texas Rangers became the first civilian force to be armed with Colt revolvers. The Texas Government bought 180 holster-sized pistols for their use. The pistols were designed for saddle-mounted rather than belt-mounted holsters. These weapons were Colt-Paterson five-shot, .44 caliber, 9-inch barrelled, revolving pistols of the type that Colt's Patent Firearms Manufacturing Company had first patented in 1836. Samuel Walker, a contemporary Ranger who rode for Captain Jack Hays, wrote to Samuel Colt in England, telling him how the rangers used his weapons. "The pistols which you made... have been in use by the Rangers for three years... In the summer of 1844, Captain J. Hays with fifteen men fought around eighty Camanche [sic] Indians, boldly attacking them on their own ground, killing and wounding about half their number... Without your pistols we would not have had the confidence to have undertaken such daring adventures."

The arrangement with Samuel Colt to manufacture a thousand Colt Whitneyville-Walker revolvers for the U.S.M.R. (United States Mounted

Right: Remember the Alamo. The "Last Stand" defense of this mission fort against overwhelming Mexican forces took place in 1836. This was the year in which Texas declared itself to be an independent republic. The defense of the Alamo became a patriotic symbol of American resistance to the domination of foreign powers.

Above: The Colt Paterson revolver that the Texas Rangers used during Captain Jack Hay's historic skirmish with the Comanche. It was a five-shot .44 caliber pistol.

Rifles) led by Captain Samuel Walker, finally established Colt's company.

The American army's Mounted Rifles were also known by the European name of "Dragoons" and the Whitneyville-Walker eventually assumed the same nomenclature. The Whitneyville-Walker was a six-shot, .44 caliber weapon with a 9-inch barrel and an overall length of fifteen and a half inches. It weighed no less than four pounds nine ounces. The excessive weight of the gun together with reliability problems led to the development of a revised version of the weapon: the Colt Dragoon, or Model 1848. Twenty thousand examples were produced for government service between 1848 and 1860, with more manufactured for sale on the civilian market. So this popular model provided plenty of work for the Colt factory.

All Colt Dragoons could take six .44 caliber rounds in an un-fluted cylinder. Many of these barrels were engraved with battle scenes and were clearly marked "U.S. DRAGOONS." The gun was a single-action revolver, with a 7.5-inch barrel and had an overall length of fourteen inches. In this revised version of the gun, its weight was reduced to four pounds. The Colt Dragoon was very robust. The barrel was keyed to the chamber axis pin and supported by a solid lug that was keyed to the lower frame. The Dragoon was manufactured in three production runs which differed in only minor details, although these differences are of immense importance to today's historians and collectors. The first model is distinguished by the oval-shaped notches on the cylinder. The second model has rectangular notches. Seven thousand first model

Below: Captain Samuel Walker of the U.S.M.R. who helped Colt to develop the improved Dragoon Model.

Dragoon revolvers were made between 1848 and 1850, but the most successful model was the third. Over 10,000 third model guns were made between 1851 and 1860. These can be easily identified by the round trigger-guard as the trigger-guards of the two previous models were square-backed.

Below: The Colt Dragoon 1st Model seen from both sides. This model can be readily identified by the square-backed trigger guard.

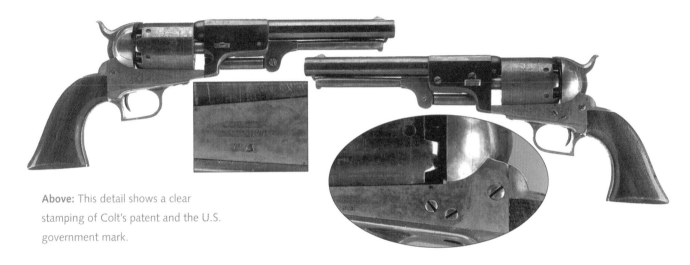

Above: This detail shows a clear stamping of Colt's patent and the U.S. government mark.

Above: The .31 caliber Baby Dragoon was developed for the civilian market and proved an instant success. Some 15,500 were produced and sold from 1848-1850.

Above: The Colt Dragoon 3rd Model had a fully-rounded trigger guard and a longer 8-inch barrel.

A HISTORY OF COLT'S PATENT FIREARMS MANUFACTURING COMPANY

Above: Colt's founder, Samuel Colt, was a man of enterprise and vision who never lived to see some of the finest guns his company would produce.

In 1832 the eighteen-year-old Samuel Colt filed his first patent application for a revolving cylinder gun. His family were wealthy citizens of Paterson, New Jersey and it was here that the first Colt factory was founded in 1837.

Despite the company's initial success in supplying the Texas Rangers with the Paterson Model, quality control problems and issues of part interchangeability led to the demise of Colt's first enterprise in 1842. But by 1846 the demand for revolvers from Samuel Walker and the Texas Rangers who were then embroiled in the Mexican War enabled Colt to re-launch the company and relocate to Hartford, Connecticut.

From the beginning Colt firearms had the marketing advantages of having pleasing aesthetic lines and a comfortable, ergonomic feel. Even the Colt name, meaning a spirited young horse, conjured up images of the untamed West. It also seemed to symbolize lively potential of America as a young and developing nation.

Colt rigorously defended his patent for revolving firearms, which delivered a monopoly in this market that lasted until 1857. By this time, the Civil War was brewing. There is nothing like the prospect of war to

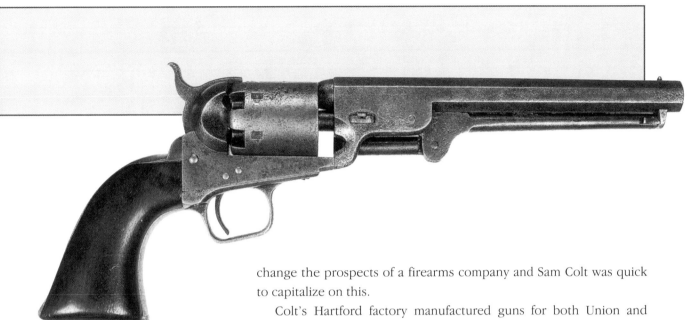

change the prospects of a firearms company and Sam Colt was quick to capitalize on this.

Colt's Hartford factory manufactured guns for both Union and Confederate forces and supplied both sides without favor. Colt was a capitalist and saw that the Civil War would offer massive opportunities for the sale of his firearms. The company had already sold weapons to both the Russian and British forces in the Crimean War and pursued the same policy in the domestic conflict. Colt even considered building an armory in the South to supply the Confederacy with Colt weapons. He continued to sell revolvers to the southern forces after the war began and sold 2,000 revolvers to the Confederate agent John Forsyth as late as 1862. However this policy led to a great deal of negative publicity for Colt. He was labeled a southern sympathizer by both the *New York Daily Tribune* and the *New York Times*. By definition this meant that he was being accused of being a traitor to the Union. To try to overcome this negative image, Colt became a Colonel in the Union army in 1861 and formed his own regiment: The 1st Regiment Colt's Revolving Rifles of Connecticut. Of course, the regiment was kitted out with the latest Colt revolving rifles. However the unit never took to the field and Colt was discharged from duty on June 20, 1861. Sadly Samuel Colt never saw the outcome of the War as he died of gout in the following year of 1862, but the momentum of his fervent belief in revolving arms propelled the company forward ever after.

In 1864 a devastating fire at the Hartford Armory destroyed much of the factory and with it Colt's productivity. Production of the Model 1861 Army Revolver dropped from 65,000 units in 1864 to just 3,000 guns in 1865. This disaster coincided with the end of the Civil War and a much depressed arms market.

Above: The Colt Model 1851 Navy. This gun became one of the company's most successful and best-selling weapons. Sales were stimulated by the start of the Civil War.

Far left: Colt's first factory at Paterson, New Jersey. The armory operated from 1836 to 1842.

Left: The Colt factory at Hartford, Connecticut. The "Onion Dome" that can be seen at the left of the photograph was built by Colt to commemorate his introduction to the court of Czar Nicolas I in 1854. Colt supplied both sides (the Russians and the British) in the Crimean War.

However, the Colt's Patent Firearms Manufacturing Company soon recovered from the fire at the Hartford Armory. Led by Samuel Colt's widow Elizabeth, who had substantial means and a large insurance on the property, the board of directors was persuaded to not only rebuild the factory but to substantially enlarge the original plant. Elizabeth Colt appointed Civil War veteran Union Major General William B. Franklin as vice president of the company on the death of her husband's right-hand man Elisha K. Root. This provided the company with a continuity of leadership that endured until 1888.

Above: Just before the end of the Civil War in 1864, the Colt factory was gutted by fire. Productivity was sharply reduced just as the flow of orders from the war ended.

THE ROLLIN WHITE PATENT

Colt's slowness to adopt cartridge firing weapons came as a direct result of Samuel Colt's own stubbornness. Cartridge firing guns such as the Spencer and the Henry were already in use during the Civil War while Colt arms still used the front-loading percussion system. Colt's belief in the efficacy of his own guns and the huge effort he invested in protecting his patents led him to miss a great opportunity to modernize his products. Colt's mistake was to dismiss a brilliant design conceived by one of his own gunsmiths, Rollin White. White conceived the idea of a bored-through revolver cylinder that could use rear-loading metallic cartridges. Colt was notorious for dismissing ideas that he hadn't had himself and for ignoring his employee's suggestions for improvements. He took Rollin White's well-meant proposals as a criticism of his designs and cancelled White's contract of employment.

As a direct result of his dismissal Rollin White took his idea to Colt's competitor, Smith & Wesson. Founded by partners Horace Smith and Daniel B. Wesson in 1852 as the Volcanic Repeating Arms Company, Smith & Wesson were quick to spot the potential of White's design. They acquired the patent for his invention and prevented Colt from being able to manufacture cartridge firearms until the early 1870s.

When Colt was finally able to compete in this market almost a decade after Samuel Colt's death, Colt factory employees William Mason and C.B. Richards designed a new cartridge firing revolver to compete with the Smith & Wesson.

The Colt Single Action Army Model 1873 is perhaps the best-known of all Colt revolvers. As the result of winning the United States government service revolver trials of 1872, the gun was adopted as America's standard military service revolver until 1892.

Colt firearms continued to be successful throughout the period of frontier expansion and the Colt Single Action revolver also played a decisive role in the Indian Wars. It became a favorite weapon for gunfighters, cowboys, and western lawmen. Ironically, it earned the title of "Peacemaker" as well as being credited as "the gun that won the West."

In a period of history when guns were vital for both personal protection and for carving out the western frontier, the Colt Single Action revolver epitomized the immortal phrase that "God made man, but Colonel Colt made them equal."

Above: William Mason was an important member of the Colt team who took the company forward in an engineering capacity after Colt's death.

Below: The Colt Single-Action revolver of 1873 was one of the company's most iconic handguns.

THE CIVIL WAR

Above: A Federal cavalryman with a brace of Colt Army pistols in his belt.

The American Civil War was a devastating event that tore apart the original European settlers of America. Its effects were felt for years, even after it had ended. Its impact created a climate where firearms became essential equipment for a generation of Americans. Many men learnt the use of guns and had become proficient in handling them during their war service. The feeling of coming close to death in daily fire fights spawned a tough and reckless breed of man who would risk everything to protect their land, pride, prestige, and power. Inevitably, once this type of man was discharged from military service, they were drawn to the opportunities offered by the emerging western frontier. Most of the Civil War troops took their guns home with them and many of these were to see service on the frontier.

Guns themselves evolved at a tremendous pace over the course of the Civil War. The conflict began with the use of single-shot, muzzle-loading weapons but ended with the use of multi-shot repeating firearms.

HANDGUNS

Even before the Civil War, the handgun was seen as an essential personal defense tool for the traveler, householder, settler, and cowhand, especially in the more lawless regions of the West. So when men flocked to enlist in military service, many brought their own pistols and revolvers. Some would be used as a main fighting weapon or were kept as a handy backup for use in a crisis. The rapidly expanding armies struggled to provide their men with anything like enough weapons, so any available firearms were pressed into service. Enterprising businessmen on both sides set up factories both large and small to fill the gaps in supply. Sometimes these armories simply copied the best designs available. Overseas manufacturers were also quick to spot the opportunity, and many guns flowed into America from Britain and Europe.

So, while the popular image of the Civil War forces may be of men

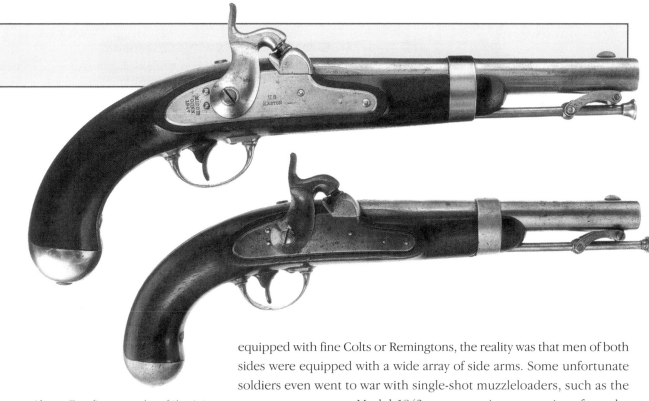

Above: Two fine examples of the Aston Model 1842 pistol which was still being issued at the outset of the war.

Below: The Nepperhan Fire Arms Company made about 5,000 of these .31 Colt copies during the Civil War.

equipped with fine Colts or Remingtons, the reality was that men of both sides were equipped with a wide array of side arms. Some unfortunate soldiers even went to war with single-shot muzzleloaders, such as the government pattern Model 1842, or percussion conversions from the earlier flintlock Model 1836.

However, the majority of fighting men were equipped with some form of percussion revolver. Some had cartridge revolvers, and a few even had early repeating magazine pistols.

The revolver had first come into widespread use in the middle of the nineteenth century. Some gun manufacturers had created earlier

Above: Many of the advanced double–action Beaumont-Adams revolvers were imported from England during the Civil War.

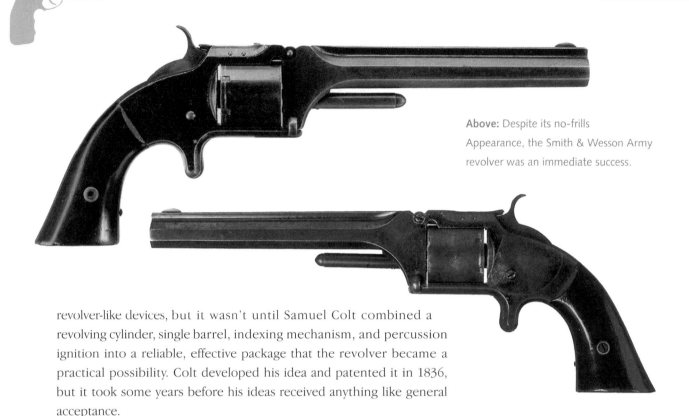

Above: Despite its no-frills Appearance, the Smith & Wesson Army revolver was an immediate success.

Above: Its six-round cylinder was chambered for metal rimfire cartridges.

revolver-like devices, but it wasn't until Samuel Colt combined a revolving cylinder, single barrel, indexing mechanism, and percussion ignition into a reliable, effective package that the revolver became a practical possibility. Colt developed his idea and patented it in 1836, but it took some years before his ideas received anything like general acceptance.

Colt's patent expired in 1856, allowing others to manufacture directly competitive weapons, but it took the outbreak of war to really put the revolver on the map. Manufacturers sprung up on all sides, some with their own designs and some producing straightforward Colt copies.

At the outbreak of war most American-made revolvers were single-action, so the user had to manually cock the weapon, usually by thumbing back the hammer, which also positioned the cylinder. All the user then had to do was aim the gun and pull the trigger to fire. This system made for a relatively slow rate of fire, but it did mean that carefully aimed shots were easier. Single-action mechanisms are also simple with very little to break or go wrong. This was a popular feature for users who could be hundreds of miles away from the nearest gunsmith. Self-cocking revolvers were more popular in Britain and Europe, where the user simply had to apply a single pull on the trigger to cock and fire the weapon. The ability to fire quick snapshots was seen as useful in a close-range brawl but the downside of this system was that accurate long-range fire was less easy.

Eventually the double-action lock was invented, giving the option of both methods of firing the gun. The best-known double-action design was that of Britain's Robert Adams and Lieutenant Beaumont. This revolver and many other British imports were used widely in the war.

Opposite: A Union Officer fires his Smith & Wesson Model No.2 Army revolver into the melee at Alatoona Pass. In the background Union troops are firing their Henry rifles.

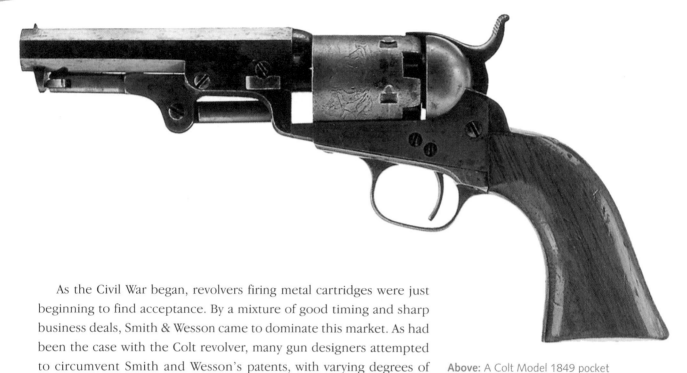

Above: A Colt Model 1849 pocket revolver with a 4-inch barrel. Many of these weapons were privately purchased for use in the war.

Opposite: Major Hill of the 45th Ohio Volunteer Infantry holds his saber and has his Colt Navy stuffed into his belt.

As the Civil War began, revolvers firing metal cartridges were just beginning to find acceptance. By a mixture of good timing and sharp business deals, Smith & Wesson came to dominate this market. As had been the case with the Colt revolver, many gun designers attempted to circumvent Smith and Wesson's patents, with varying degrees of success.

What were all these handguns used for? Only effective at very close range and after constant practise, handguns were completely overshadowed by long arms in large-scale battle. But handguns were particularly useful to two groups of soldier. Officers needed to be highly visible in battle, and often used their swords to draw attention to themselves and signal orders to their men. They needed their hands unencumbered, and a handgun provided the ideal compromise of firepower and portability. In this case the sidearm was also seen as a badge of rank, differentiating between commanders and their men.

Revolvers were also extensively used by mounted soldiers. Cavalry troops needed a weapon that could be aimed and fired with one hand, and one that didn't need to be reloaded after every shot.

But many other soldiers also used handguns. It was not uncommon to see a rifle-equipped infantryman who also had a pistol stuffed into his waistband in case of emergency. In practice these were rarely used, but they did provide a degree of comfort as Billy Yank and Johnny Reb marched off to war.

Colt Navy Model 1851

The Colt Model 1851 Navy revolver was one of the most popular handguns ever made, with some 215,000 manufactured in various Colt factories in 1850 through 1873. It has a 7.5-inch octagonal barrel and a smooth sided cylinder which houses six .36 caliber rounds. In most cases, the cylinder was decorated with a scene involving a naval battle between United States and Mexican fleets. It was this decoration that gave the type its "Navy" designation, and the term ended up being used to describe any military percussion revolver in .36 caliber. Revolvers made for .44 rounds were usually called "Army." Many fighting men, whether on land or at sea, preferred the lighter weight and smaller size of the .36, and revolvers of both sizes were used by all branches of the armed forces, whether Federal or Confederate.

COLT NAVY MODEL 1851	
TYPE: PERCUSSION REVOLVER	
ORIGIN: COLT PFA MFG. CO., HARTFORD, CONNECTICUT	
CALIBER: .36	
BARREL LENGTH: 7.5 INCHES	

Above: This revolver is a standard U.S. Navy-issue version of the gun, marked "USN" on the butt.

Right: This Model 1851 was presented to Major Hill of the 45th Regiment, Ohio Volunteer Infantry. The inset shows the high standard of finish applied to weapons intended for sale on the open market.

A shoulder stock was available for the Model 1851, which could be attached to the butt for more accurate long-range shooting. The company applied three different forms of address on these revolvers, some being marked "Saml. Colt New York City," while others bore "Saml. Colt Hartford, Ct;" and there was a yet further variation of "Saml. Colt New York U.S. America."

Brooklyn Bridge Colt Copy

Successful weapons were often copied by other manufacturers, either to make a quick profit in peacetime or to create effective weapons as quickly as possible for the fighting armies. Colt's revolvers were probably imitated more than any other manufacturer's, and this one is typical of the many copies that were made of the Colt Pocket series (see later entry). Almost identical to Colt's production, it has a scene of ships under a bridge engraved on the cylinder.

BROOKLYN BRIDGE COLT COPY	
TYPE: FIVE-ROUND, PERCUSSION REVOLVER	
ORIGIN: UNKNOWN	
CALIBER: .38	
BARREL LENGTH: 4 INCHES	

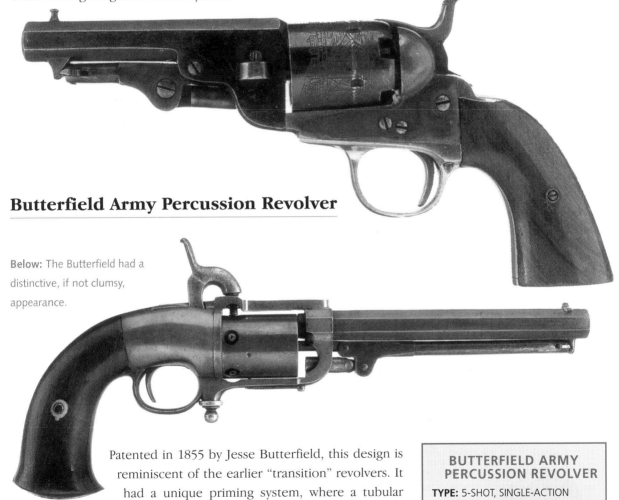

Butterfield Army Percussion Revolver

Below: The Butterfield had a distinctive, if not clumsy, appearance.

Patented in 1855 by Jesse Butterfield, this design is reminiscent of the earlier "transition" revolvers. It had a unique priming system, where a tubular magazine (accessed from in front of the trigger guard) held paper "pellet-style" percussion primers. When the single-action hammer was cocked, a pellet was slid over the cylinder nipple at the firing position. The Butterfield was ordered in small numbers by the US government, but the contract was canceled after only about 600 were delivered. A few saw service on both sides during the war.

BUTTERFIELD ARMY PERCUSSION REVOLVER	
TYPE: 5-SHOT, SINGLE-ACTION PERCUSSION REVOLVER	
ORIGIN: JESSE BUTTERFIELD, PHILADELPHIA, PENNSYLVANIA	
CALIBER: .41	
BARREL LENGTH: 7 INCHES	

Colt Model 1855 Root Revolver

This design was developed by a Colt employee, Elijah Root, and was the company's first ever solid-frame design, with a top-strap across the cylinder joining the barrel and frame. It was fitted with a side-mounted hammer, a stud-trigger without guard, and a single-action lock. It was produced in .28 and .31 calibers, but all have a 3.5-inch barrel. It is very popular with modern gun-collectors, who know it simply as "the Root," and who have identified no less than twelve minor variations in the actual production weapons.

Below: A Root Model 2, complete with Colt's address on the barrel.

Below: Another Root, this time a Model 7. This had a screw to hold the cylinder-pin in place.

Above: At some point in its history this gun has been modified by one of its owners and incorporates some replacement parts.

COLT MODEL 1855 ROOT REVOLVER

TYPE: SIX-SHOT, SINGLE-ACTION, SIDE-HAMMER REVOLVER

ORIGIN: COLT PFA MFG CO., HARTFORD, CONNECTICUT

CALIBER: .28 OR .31

BARREL LENGTH: 3.5 INCHES

Colt Model 1860 Army

The production figures for the Colt Model 1860 are self-explanatory – the total produced between 1860 and 1873 was 200,500, of which the U.S. government accepted no less than 127,156. Designed as the successor to the Third Model Dragoon (see earlier), it became one of the most widely used of all handguns during the Civil War and was equally popular in both the Union and Confederate armies.

It was a percussion revolver, with rammer loading from the front of the cylinder and any reasonably experienced shooter ensured that he had a stock of paper cartridges close at hand for rapid reloading. The weapon weighed 2.74 pounds and was fitted with either a 7.5-in or 8-in barrel.

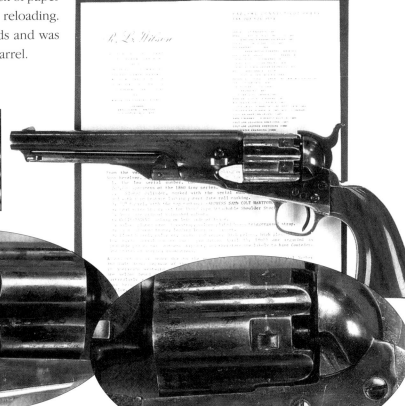

COLT MODEL 1860 ARMY	
TYPE: PERCUSSION REVOLVER	
ORIGIN: COLT PFA MFG. CO., HARTFORD, CONNECTICUT	
CALIBER: .44	
BARREL LENGTH: 7.5 INCHES AND 8 INCHES	

Above: Here is a very early production example, bearing the serial number "360." The weapon has a fluted cylinder and 7.5-in barrel, and, considering its age, is in remarkably good condition. In addition to all that, there is accompanying evidence that the original owner was Mr. N. Nickerson of Canton, New York and the provenance is certified in the letter, shown here, from R.L. Wilson, a renowned expert on Colt handguns.

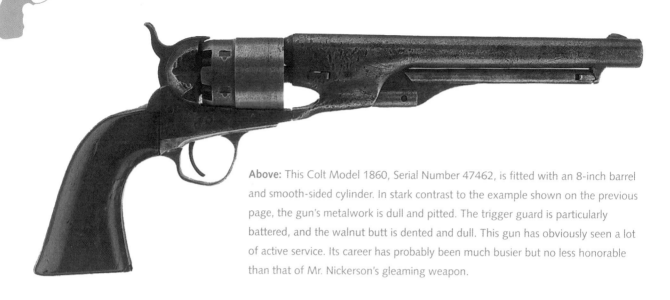

Above: This Colt Model 1860, Serial Number 47462, is fitted with an 8-inch barrel and smooth-sided cylinder. In stark contrast to the example shown on the previous page, the gun's metalwork is dull and pitted. The trigger guard is particularly battered, and the walnut butt is dented and dull. This gun has obviously seen a lot of active service. Its career has probably been much busier but no less honorable than that of Mr. Nickerson's gleaming weapon.

Colt Model 1861 Navy

Colt also updated the Model 1851 Navy, using a similar smoothly shaped barrel and rammer shroud to that of the Model 1860 Army. The ensuing design is an elegant and visually appealing weapon with a 7.5-inch barrel and a smooth-sided cylinder housing six shots. Some 39,000 were made, and through its lifetime there were remarkably few variations on the Model 1861.

Right: Sergeant Stephen Clinton (right) poses with a comrade from the Sixth Virginia Cavalry. Clinton has a large Colt .44in Army revolver in his belt, while the second man has a smaller Colt, probably a Model 1849.

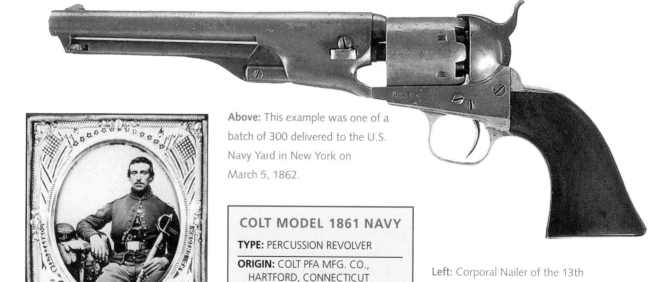

Above: This example was one of a batch of 300 delivered to the U.S. Navy Yard in New York on March 5, 1862.

COLT MODEL 1861 NAVY	
TYPE: PERCUSSION REVOLVER	
ORIGIN: COLT PFA MFG. CO., HARTFORD, CONNECTICUT	
CALIBER: .36	
BARREL LENGTH: 7.5 INCHES	

Left: Corporal Nailer of the 13th Pennsylvania Cavalry poses with his sword by his side and Colt Navy in his belt.

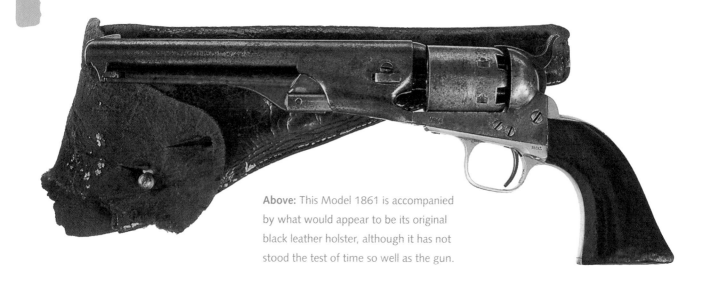

Above: This Model 1861 is accompanied by what would appear to be its original black leather holster, although it has not stood the test of time so well as the gun.

Colt Model 1862 Pocket Navy

Colt manufactured some 19,000 of these revolvers, which were, in essence, a smaller version of the Model 1851 Navy, chambered for .36 caliber and with a five-shot, smooth-sided cylinder decorated with a roll-on engraving of a Western stage-coach hold-up. The barrels were 4.5, 5.5, or 6.5 inches in length, with the loading-lever attached underneath. The example shown here has a 5.5-inch barrel and is in very good condition.

Below: The engraving of a coach hold-up on the cylinder indicates that the gun was being marketed for self-defense.

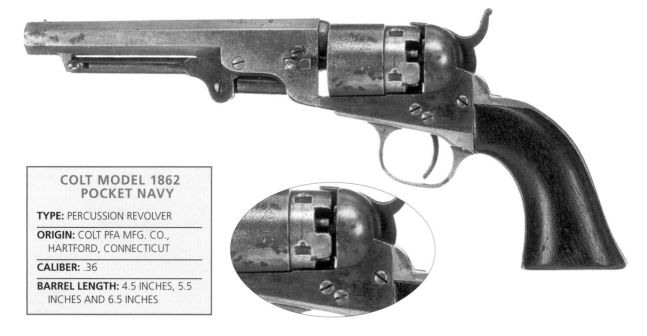

COLT MODEL 1862 POCKET NAVY
TYPE: PERCUSSION REVOLVER
ORIGIN: COLT PFA MFG. CO., HARTFORD, CONNECTICUT
CALIBER: .36
BARREL LENGTH: 4.5 INCHES, 5.5 INCHES AND 6.5 INCHES

Eagle Arms Cup-Primer Revolver

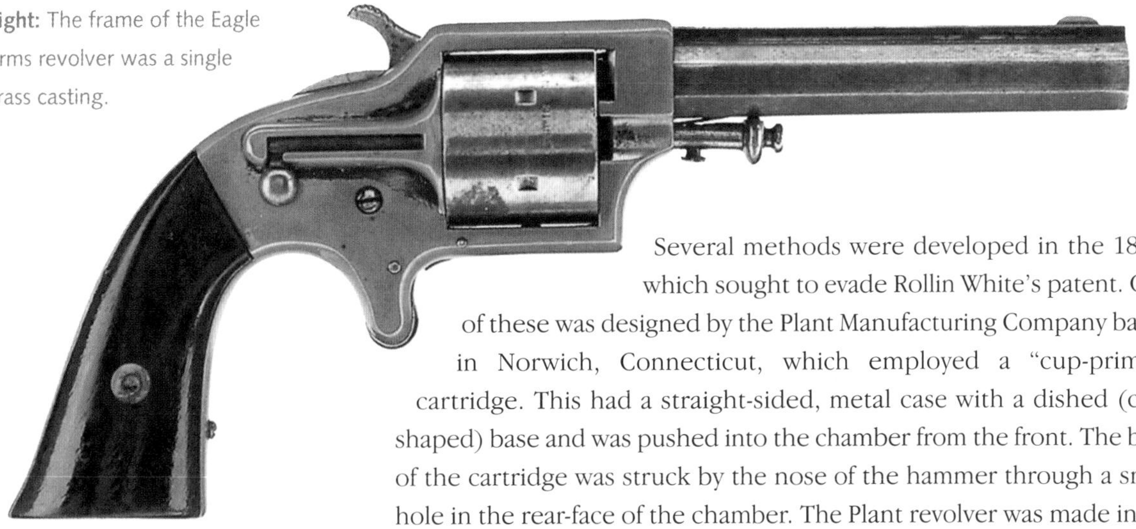

Right: The frame of the Eagle Arms revolver was a single brass casting.

Several methods were developed in the 1860s which sought to evade Rollin White's patent. One of these was designed by the Plant Manufacturing Company based in Norwich, Connecticut, which employed a "cup-primer" cartridge. This had a straight-sided, metal case with a dished (cup-shaped) base and was pushed into the chamber from the front. The base of the cartridge was struck by the nose of the hammer through a small hole in the rear-face of the chamber. The Plant revolver was made in .41 and .36 caliber, but the Eagle Arms Company produced the smaller version, seen here in .31 caliber (Eagle Arms was another brand name used by the Johnson & Bye company). This revolver had a 3.5-inch barrel, smooth-sided cylinder and spur trigger. The slot which can be seen behind the cylinder houses the ejector-rod which was pushed forward through the hammer-aperture in rear of each cylinder to eject the empty cartridge case forward.

EAGLE ARMS CUP-PRIMER REVOLVER

TYPE: FIVE-ROUND, DOUBLE-ACTION, CUP-PRIMER REVOLVER

ORIGIN: JOHNSON, BYE & COMPANY, WORCESTER, MASSACHUSETTS

CALIBER: .31

BARREL LENGTH: 3.5 INCHES

Hammond Bulldog Pistol

A single shot self-defense weapon in the deringer class, this crudely finished breechloading pistol fired a powerful .44 cartridge and was patented in 1864. It would be effective enough at close range, and pistols of this nature became popular with many soldiers in the Civil War, who bought them to carry as concealed last-ditch back-up weapons.

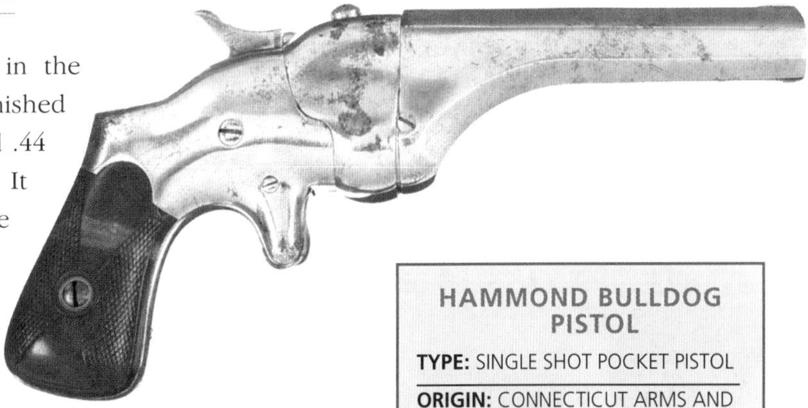

Above: This example appears to have survived with much of its original nickel finish.

HAMMOND BULLDOG PISTOL

TYPE: SINGLE SHOT POCKET PISTOL

ORIGIN: CONNECTICUT ARMS AND MANUFACTURING COMPANY

CALIBER: .44

BARREL LENGTH: 4 INCHES

Manhattan Navy

The Manhattan firearms company were one of the many who began manufacturing revolvers when Colt's patent expired. Their main products were copies of the Model 1851 Navy and Model 1949 pocket series, and were so close that Colt took legal action to have production stopped. Even so, over 80,000 Manhattan revolvers were made.

Below: A Manhattan Navy model, which has features from both the Colt Navy and pocket revolvers.

Below: Manhattan products were well-made and often finely decorated. This engraved .36 Navy model has a 4-inch barrel.

MANHATTAN NAVY	
TYPE: FIVE-SHOT PERCUSSION REVOLVER	
ORIGIN: MANHATTAN FIREARMS CO., NEWARK, NEW JERSEY	
CALIBER: .36	
BARREL LENGTH: 5 INCHES	

Manhattan Tip-up

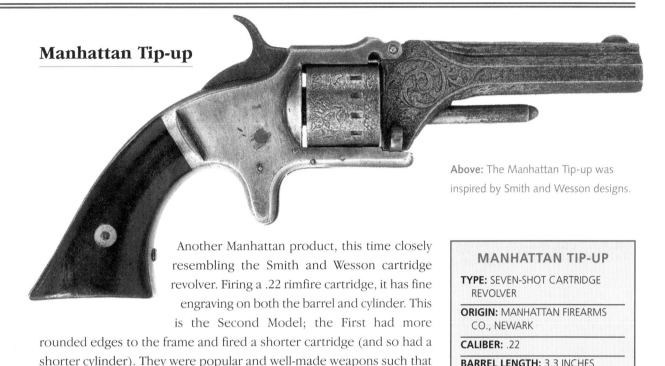

Above: The Manhattan Tip-up was inspired by Smith and Wesson designs.

Another Manhattan product, this time closely resembling the Smith and Wesson cartridge revolver. Firing a .22 rimfire cartridge, it has fine engraving on both the barrel and cylinder. This is the Second Model; the First had more rounded edges to the frame and fired a shorter cartridge (and so had a shorter cylinder). They were popular and well-made weapons such that over 17,000 were made before a lawsuit stopped production.

MANHATTAN TIP-UP
TYPE: SEVEN-SHOT CARTRIDGE REVOLVER
ORIGIN: MANHATTAN FIREARMS CO., NEWARK
CALIBER: .22
BARREL LENGTH: 3.3 INCHES

Massachusetts Arms Co. Dragoon Percussion Revolver

The Massachusetts Army Company operated at Chicopee Falls, Massachusetts from 1849 to 1876, during which time it produced rifles and revolvers under licence from other patent-holders. One such was Daniel Leavitt of Cabotsville whose design was produced first by Wesson, Stevens & Miller at Hartford, and subsequently by the Massachusetts Arms Co., and is now commonly known as the "Wesson and Leavitt." This example, made in the early 1850s, shows the good finish and neat design.

MASSACHUSETTS ARMS CO. DRAGOON PERCUSSION REVOLVER
TYPE: PERCUSSION REVOLVER
ORIGIN: MASSACHUSETTS ARMS COMPANY, CHICOPEE FALLS, MASSACHUSETTS
CALIBER: .40
BARREL LENGTH: 71 INCHES

Above: The gun is solidly engineered with a forged sidehammer and underslung cylinder.

Metropolitan Navy Percussion

When the Colt factory was damaged by fire in 1864, the Metropolitan Arms Co. began to manufacture copies of Colt weapons. This "Navy" model is almost indistinguishable from the Colt original of the time, even down to the faint remnants of the naval battle scene engraved on the cylinder. It also has a brass trigger guard with walnut grips.

METROPOLITAN NAVY PERCUSSION	
TYPE: SIX-SHOT SINGLE-ACTION REVOLVER	
ORIGIN: METROPOLITAN ARMS CO., NEW YORK	
CALIBER: .36	
BARREL LENGTH: 7.5 INCHES	

Below: A fine example of this Colt lookalike.

National No. 2 Deringer

Moore's Patent Firearms Co. was established in Brooklyn in the middle of the nineteenth century and changed its name to the National Arms Company in 1866. Among its products was the No. 1 Deringer, which was very successful, achieving sales of some 10,000 in 1860–65. This was followed by an improved model which had just entered production when the name changed and was then marketed as the National No. 2 Deringer (seen here). The No.2 Deringer had a spur trigger and was reloaded by pressing the release catch and swivelling the barrel to expose the chamber. The National Arms Co. was bought by Colt in 1870, following which this weapon continued to be marketed as the Colt No. 2 Deringer.

NATIONAL NO. 2 DERINGER	
TYPE: DERINGER-TYPE POCKET PISTOL	
ORIGIN: NATIONAL ARMS CO., BROOKLYN, NEW YORK	
CALIBER: .41	
BARREL LENGTH: 2.5 INCHES	

Perrin Centerfire Revolver

In 1859, Perrin & Delmas patented the first European centerfire revolver and produced a successful range of weapons. The large European-style centerfire revolver shown here was one of the many foreign weapons that found their way into the hands of American fighting men during the Civil War. Some 550 or so were purchased by the Federal Government and others were bought privately. A heavy and powerful enough weapon, it must have been difficult for an American owner to find a reliable supply of the eleven mm centerfire cartridges it used.

PERRIN CENTERFIRE REVOLVER
TYPE: SIX-ROUND, CENTERFIRE CARTRIDGE REVOLVER
ORIGIN: L. PERRIN ET CIE, PARIS, FRANCE
CALIBER: .11 MM
BARREL LENGTH: 6 INCHES

Pettengill Army Model

Although this revolver was designed and named after Charles Pettengill, it was actually manufactured by Rogers, Spencer and Co. Pettengill designed the self-cocking firing mechanism, with the hammer completely enclosed within the frame. The firer just pulled the trigger to index the cartridge and raise then drop the hammer. There was no provision for single-action fire, and the heavy trigger force made it difficult to shoot accurately. The Pettengill was the subject of a 5,000 item order from the U.S. Ordnance Department in 1861, but had to be modified when the first batch was rejected as unsuitable. Eventually only some 2,000 of the modified weapon were delivered.

PETTENGILL ARMY MODEL
TYPE: SIX-SHOT SELF-COCKING REVOLVER
ORIGIN: ROGERS, SPENCER & CO., WILLOW DALE, NEW YORK
CALIBER: .44
BARREL LENGTH: 6.5 INCHES

Above: This pistol looked awkward -- and was equally awkward to use.

Remington-Beals Navy Revolver

By the end of the 1850s Remington was producing a range of pocket revolvers, pistols, and rifles, but had no weapons in the larger "military" calibers. In 1858 Fordyce Beals took the principles of his third model and developed an entirely new arm in .36 caliber. It had a large solid frame, complete with integral top strap, octagonal barrel and single-action lock. A large hinged ram sat beneath the barrel. This turned out to be a reliable and effective weapon, and was ordered by the U.S. Government as they rearmed in preparation for the Civil War. The first government deliveries to see service were actually the .44 Army version.

REMINGTON-BEALS NAVY REVOLVER	
TYPE: SIX-SHOT SINGLE-ACTION REVOLVER	
ORIGIN: REMINGTON ARMORY, ILION, NEW YORK	
CALIBER: .36	
BARREL LENGTH: 7 INCHES	

Above: A nicely preserved example in its original blued finish.

Remington-Beals Army Revolver

When Col. Ripley, the Chief of Ordnance, examined the Remington-Beals Navy prototypes, he immediately placed a large order – but for revolvers in .44 Army caliber. This revolver has a similar appearance to the original .36 version but is slightly larger and has a longer barrel. The first deliveries were made in August 1862; the first of a long line of Remington large caliber percussion revolvers.

Above: 5,000 of these guns were ordered by the Federal authorities at the outset of the war. Each gun cost $15.

PERRIN CENTERFIRE REVOLVER	
TYPE: SIX-SHOT SINGLE-ACTION REVOLVER	
ORIGIN: REMINGTON ARMORY, ILION, NEW YORK	
CALIBER: .44	
BARREL LENGTH: 8 INCHES	

Remington Model 1861 Army Revolver

Soon after the Remington-Beals military revolvers entered production, the company looked to improve the design. The main difference was a modification to the way the cylinder axle pin was retained. A channel was cut in the top of the rammer arm to allow the pin to be removed easily. The system was patented by Dr. Elliott and the weapon is sometimes referred to as the Model 1861 Elliott's Patent Army Revolver. In service conditions this system was found to be too fragile, and many revolvers had a small screw added to block this channel.

The Model 1861 is also known as the "Old Model Army." It had a distinctive outline, with an integral top strap, large gap in front of the lower edge of the cylinder, and a long sloping web on the loading ram under the barrel. This form set the pattern for all subsequent Remington military percussion revolvers.

Solid, reliable, and popular, thousands were made and used during the Civil War and after. Many were manufactured at the Remington facility at Utica created to meet the demands of the war, although they bear "Remington, Ilion" markings.

REMINGTON MODEL 1861 ARMY REVOLVER	
TYPE: SIX-SHOT SINGLE-ACTION REVOLVER	
ORIGIN: REMINGTON ARMORY, ILION AND UTICA, NEW YORK	
CALIBER: .44	
BARREL LENGTH: 8 INCHES	

Above: The Remington Model 1861 Army revolver was one of the most popular and commonly used revolvers of the war.

Remington Model 1861 Navy Revolver

As with the Remington-Beals designs, a version of the Model 1861 was also produced in .36 caliber. Also referred to as the "Old Model Navy," it followed the same design as its slightly larger brethren. Just as popular as the Army model, thousands also saw hard wartime service.

REMINGTON MODEL 1861 NAVY REVOLVER	
TYPE: SIX-SHOT SINGLE-ACTION REVOLVER	
ORIGIN: REMINGTON ARMORY, ILION AND UTICA, NEW YORK	
CALIBER: .36	
BARREL LENGTH: 7.42 INCHES	

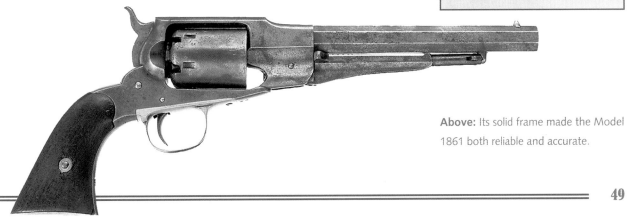

Above: Its solid frame made the Model 1861 both reliable and accurate.

Remington New Model Army Revolver

Wartime experience showed some weaknesses in Remington's Model 1861, especially concerning the cylinder fixing system. Remington modified the design by improving the fixing pin and adding safety notches around the rear edge of the cylinder. The end result was one of the finest percussion revolvers ever and the only one to really challenge Colt's dominance of the military market. Over 120,000 were delivered during the Civil War, and at its peak, production reached over 1,000 a week.

Of course, a version of the New Model was made in .36 Navy caliber, but this didn't sell quite so well – although the 28,000 produced was still a healthy number.

Above & below: Two views of the successful New Model Army. Its great chance came when the Colt factory was largely destroyed by fire, leaving the Remington gun with little competition for the remainder of the war.

REMINGTON NEW MODEL ARMY REVOLVER

TYPE: SIX-SHOT SINGLE-ACTION REVOLVER

ORIGIN: REMINGTON ARMORY, ILION, NEW YORK

CALIBER: .44

BARREL LENGTH: 8 INCHES

Savage Navy Revolver

Edward Savage and Henry S. North started to cooperate in the early 1850s, their only known design being the "Figure-8 Revolver," so named because of the shape of the trigger. These were patented by North and some 400 were produced between 1856 and 1859. Edward Savage then formed the Savage Revolving Firearms Company in 1860 and received two known major government contracts, the first of which was for some 25,000 Model 1861 Springfield muskets. The second contract was for the revolver seen here, which was marked as being to North's patents of 1856, 1859 and 1860, and some 20,000 were produced, of which 11,284 went to the Navy. Our two examples differ in that the one shown here has a smooth cylinder, while the example on the next page has a fluted cylinder.

SAVAGE NAVY REVOLVER
TYPE: SIX-SHOT PERCUSSION REVOLVER
ORIGINS: SAVAGE REVOLVING FIREARMS CO., MIDDLETOWN, CONNECTICUT
CALIBER: .36
BARREL LENGTH: 7.1 INCHES

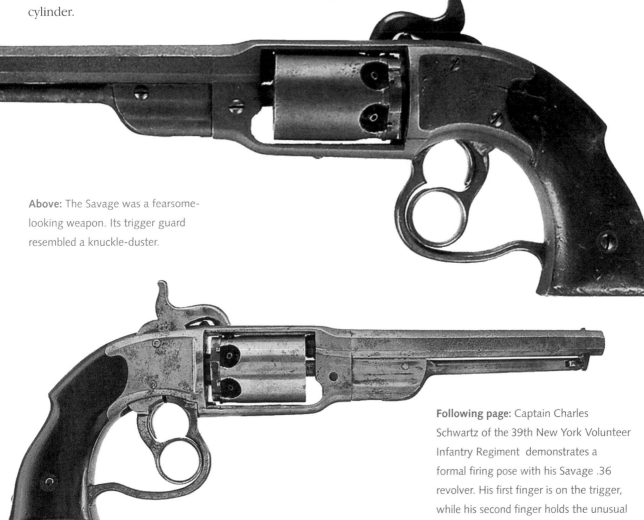

Above: The Savage was a fearsome-looking weapon. Its trigger guard resembled a knuckle-duster.

Following page: Captain Charles Schwartz of the 39th New York Volunteer Infantry Regiment demonstrates a formal firing pose with his Savage .36 revolver. His first finger is on the trigger, while his second finger holds the unusual cocking lever under the trigger.

Cooper Pocket Revolver

James Maslin Cooper was a gunsmith who was in business in Philadelphia from 1850 through 1864 and then at Frankford, Pennsylvania until 1869, when the company ceased to trade. During that time the company's products were limited to a pepperbox and various models of this percussion revolver, based on patents issued to him in 1860 and 1863. There were variants with 4-inch, 5-inch, and 6-inch barrels, but all were chambered for the .31 cartridge. It was unusual for its time in having a double-action mechanism and although some 15,000 were produced the company failed to survive. Illustrated here is an example with a 4-inch barrel and walnut grips.

COOPER POCKET REVOLVER
TYPE: SIX-CHAMBER, DOUBLE-ACTION PERCUSSION REVOLVER
ORIGIN: COOPER FIREARMS MANUFACTURING CO., PHILADELPHIA, PENNSYLVANIA
CALIBER: .31
BARREL LENGTH: 4 INCHES, 5 INCHES AND 6 INCHES

Below: The Cooper has accents of both Colt and Remington Rider pistols in its design.

Deringer M1842 Navy Pistol

Below: Another example of the Model 1842 Navy. This gun is one of a batch of 1,200 contracted to Henry Deringer.

Above: Remington's workmanship obviously wasn't up to standard, as only 300 guns were accepted by the navy.

DERINGER M1842 NAVY PISTOL	
TYPE: SIX-SHOT SINGLE-ACTION REVOLVER	
ORIGIN: REMINGTON ARMORY, ILION, NEW YORK	
CALIBER: .44	
BARREL LENGTH: 8 INCHES	

Spiller & Burr Revolver

On the outbreak of the war, two rich Virginia gentlemen, Edward N. Spiller and David J. Burr, combined with a weapons expert, James H. Burton, to establish a factory to produce a revolver for the Confederate States Army cavalry. The factory was initially sited in Richmond, Virginia, but then moved to Atlanta, Georgia and finally to Macon, also in Georgia, where it set up business in the CSA Armory. The undertaking was always hampered by the pressures of the war, shortage of materials and of skilled labor. The main contract was to deliver 15,000 revolvers in thirty months and had they succeed, Spiller, Burr and Burton would have made a very large profit; in

the event, however, only some 1,500 were completed between 1862 and 1865.

Burton's design was based on the Whitney 1858 Navy revolver, and specifically on the Second Model, First Variation, which was in production in the North at the Whitneyville factory, located outside New Haven, Connecticut. Due to shortages of material in the South, however, Burton had to adapt the design in two ways: by using iron instead of steel for the cylinder and brass instead of iron for the frame.

The example shown here shows both the strong resemblance to the Whitney and the poorer standard of finish, although there is no reason to think that it did not work as well. Some of the surviving examples are marked with the name "Spiller & Burr" and others with "C.S." (Confederate States). The story of this revolver highlights the immense industrial disadvantages facing the Confederacy in its struggle against the much better resourced North.

SPILLER & BURR REVOLVER	
TYPE: SIX-ROUND, PERCUSSION REVOLVER	
ORIGIN: SPILLER & BURR, ATLANTA, GEORGIA	
CALIBER: .36	
BARREL LENGTH: 7 INCHES	

Starr Model 1858 and 1863 Army Revolvers

The Starr Arms Company had its offices on Broadway, New York, and factories at Binghampton, Morrisania and Yonkers. The company manufactured weapons designed by Ebenezer (Eben) T. Starr and also those designed by its president, H.H. Wolcott. The company produced a number of deringers and pepperpots designed by Starr and also a very effective revolver which appeared in three models: Model 1858 Navy, Model 1858 Army Double-Action and the 1863 Single-Action Army.

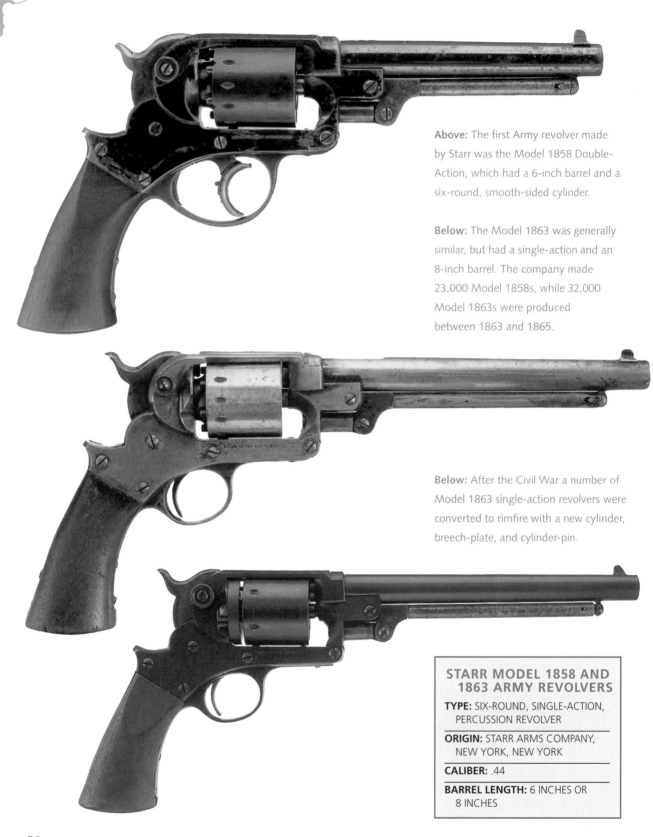

Above: The first Army revolver made by Starr was the Model 1858 Double-Action, which had a 6-inch barrel and a six-round, smooth-sided cylinder.

Below: The Model 1863 was generally similar, but had a single-action and an 8-inch barrel. The company made 23,000 Model 1858s, while 32,000 Model 1863s were produced between 1863 and 1865.

Below: After the Civil War a number of Model 1863 single-action revolvers were converted to rimfire with a new cylinder, breech-plate, and cylinder-pin.

STARR MODEL 1858 AND 1863 ARMY REVOLVERS

TYPE: SIX-ROUND, SINGLE-ACTION, PERCUSSION REVOLVER

ORIGIN: STARR ARMS COMPANY, NEW YORK, NEW YORK

CALIBER: .44

BARREL LENGTH: 6 INCHES OR 8 INCHES

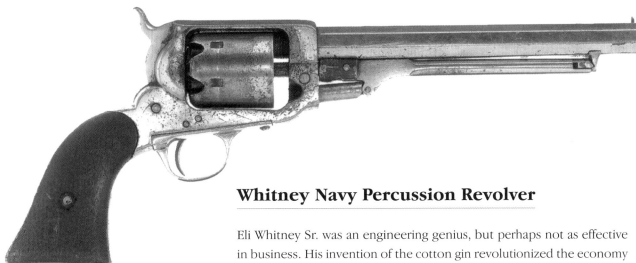

Whitney Navy Percussion Revolver

WHITNEY NAVY PERCUSSION REVOLVER

TYPE: SIX SHOT, SINGLE-ACTION PERCUSSION REVOLVER

ORIGIN: WHITNEYVILLE ARMORY, NEW HAVEN, CONNECTICUT

CALIBER: .36

BARREL LENGTH: 7.5 INCHES

Eli Whitney Sr. was an engineering genius, but perhaps not as effective in business. His invention of the cotton gin revolutionized the economy of the South, but for various reasons, including competition from other manufacturers, Whitney made very little money from it. He then turned his energies to arms manufacture, and from 1798 onwards, Whitney's company produced a range of longarms and revolvers for both government and civilian markets. Whitney's real strength was in the development of manufacturing techniques, and the company advertised itself as being the first to create standardized parts that could be assembled by workmen with little or no experience.

By the 1860s, the company was in the hands of Whitney's son, Eli Whitney Jr. Financially it was struggling, and most of its efforts were devoted to assembling and selling weapons from surplus parts bought from the government and other armories.

The Whitney company's first experience of manufacturing handguns was in 1847 when they made over 1,000 .44 caliber revolvers for Samuel Colt. At that time Colt had no facilities of his own and needed to sub-contract the manufacture of a government contract he had been awarded.

Whitney went on to develop weapons to their own design and by the late 1850s was making this series of military caliber weapons to compete with the Colt Navy types. Unlike the Colts, the Whitney revolvers had a solid frame with integral top strap above the cylinder, making for a stronger and more robust design. The one shown on the previous page is known as the second model and has an octagonal barrel, brass trigger guard and loading ram under the barrel. The Whitney Navy types proved popular in the Civil War, and over 33,000 were made.

CARBINES

As the Civil War progressed there was a growing need for special units of mounted troops to strike at weaknesses in the opposing lines. Units that began the war as traditional cavalry outfits armed with sabers changed over to pistols and carbines. The development of these new fighting skills was ideal for life on the range, herding cattle, and fighting off Indian attack. On the criminal side of things, these skills were also useful to hold up banks and stagecoaches.

Right: Henry Kelly of the 1st Battalion, 1st Virginia Cavalry embraces his Colt Revolving Carbine.

Colt Model 1855 Revolving Carbine

A reasonably rare weapon that was produced in .36, .44 and .56 inch caliber and in barrel lengths of 15, 18, 21, and 24 inches. Only 4,435 were produced and their manufacture lasted from 1856 to 1864. The .56 caliber version had a five shot cylinder and the .36 and .44 calibers were graced with six shots. This would have given the weapon a distinct advantage over single-shot carbines of the day.

This one is a "British" type, with UK proof marks, and is a .56 caliber standard carbine with military finish but without the forend and bayonet lug that would characterize it as an artillery model. Markings on the top of the frame are "Col. Colt Hartford CT. U.S.A."

The left side of the frame has a lanyard ring and the stock is typically oil-stained walnut. The cylinder is fluted and stamped "Patented Sept 10th 1855."

**COLT MODEL 1855
REVOLVING CARBINE**

TYPE: PERCUSSION REVOLVER CARBINE

ORIGIN: COLT ARMAMENTS MANUFACTURING CO., HARTFORD, CONNECTICUT

CALIBER: .36, .44 AND .56

BARREL LENGTH: 15 INCHES, 18 INCHES, 21 INCHES AND 24 INCHES

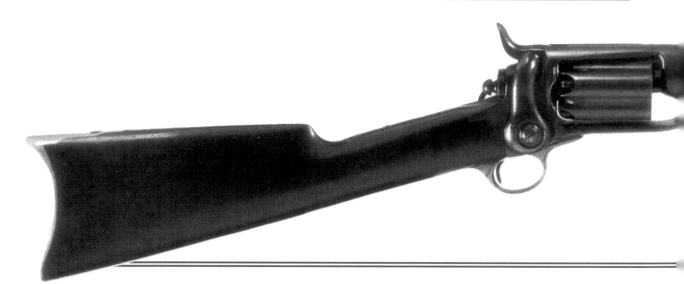

Above: The Colt Model 1855 Revolving Action appeared with different barrel lengths making it both a carbine and a rifle.

Burnside Carbine

A prolific series of Civil War carbines, the Burnside remained in production from 1857 to 1865. Designed by Ambrose E. Burnside, who at that time had formed the Bristol Firearms Co. in Rhode Island, it was later improved by one of his gunsmiths, George P. Foster. The company was also renamed the Burnside Rifle Co and moved to Providence, Rhode Island. After a faltering start, the carbine went on to great success, although most of that was after Burnside had sold his interests in the company. Burnside, of course, went on to greater things himself as the commander of the Army of the Potomac.

A short, lever-operated breechloading single-shot carbine, it used an unusual tapered cartridge cased with thin copper or foil, and had a tape primer system. The breech on the First Model is opened by a lever adjacent to the hammer, although fewer than 300 of these early examples were made in the years 1857–58.

The Second Model employs a catch inside the trigger guard to open the breech and is recognizable from later models by the lack of a forend stock. Two thousand were manufactured between 1860 and 1862. The example shown is known to have

BURNSIDE CARBINE

TYPE: PERCUSSION BREECHLOADING CARBINE

ORIGIN: BRISTOL FIREARMS CO., BRISTOL, AND BURNSIDE RIFLE CO., PROVIDENCE, BOTH RHODE ISLAND

CALIBER: .54

BARREL LENGTH: 21 INCHES

Below: The Second Model Burnside Carbine is characterized by the lack of a forend.

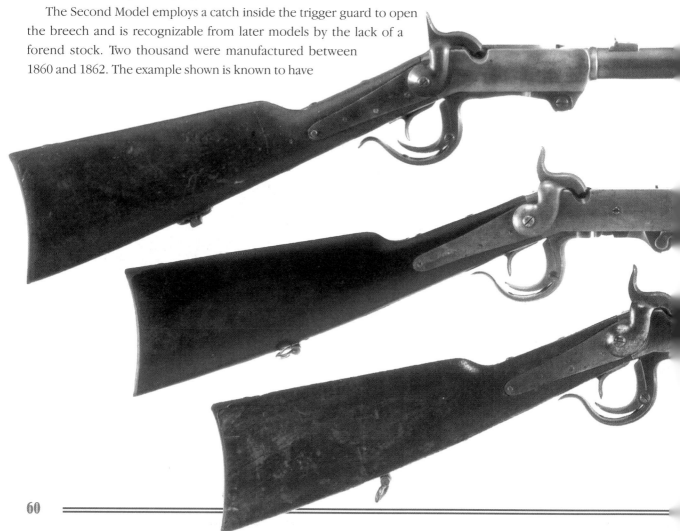

been in action at Bull Run in July 1861 in the hands of a trooper from the Rhode Island Infantry, a unit local to the factory. The Third Model used a similar breechblock to the Second Model, but had a walnut forend and metal barrel restraining band.

The Fourth Model was produced between 1862 and 1864, and was marked as the Model of 1863. It kept the barrel band and wooden forend of the Second Model, but employed a redesigned breech mechanism.

A hinged center section above the block allows for quicker and easier reloading. The Fourth Model can also sometimes be recognized by the lack of a guide screw on the right frame faceplate.

Another variant is marked as the Model of 1864 and is sometimes known as the Fifth Model. This version accounted for some 43,000 examples out of a total production run of 53,500 carbines, and are by far the most numerous of the weapons to be produced at the height of the Civil War. We show here details of the left and right sides of the frame and action, including the sliding saddle ring, the top of the breechblock and the inspector's cartouches. All finishes were originally blue.

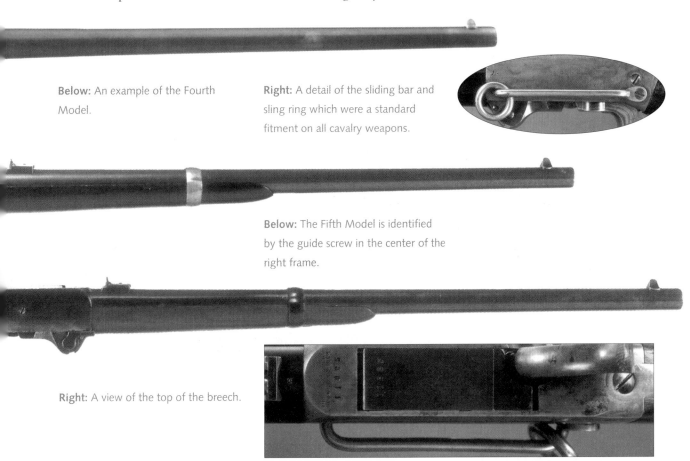

Below: An example of the Fourth Model.

Right: A detail of the sliding bar and sling ring which were a standard fitment on all cavalry weapons.

Below: The Fifth Model is identified by the guide screw in the center of the right frame.

Right: A view of the top of the breech.

Joslyn Model 1862 and 1864 Carbines

The Joslyn turned out to be one of the most prolific of Civil War arms, being produced from early in the War through to spring 1865. It evolved during that time from percussion cap ignition to .52 rimfire ammunition in the early 1862 model, with the nipple giving way to the firing pin. Union Cavalry units equipped with the Joslyn were the 4th and 8th Indiana, 19th New York, 13th Tennessee, 9th Pennsylvania, 3rd West Virginia, 2nd Wisconsin, 1st Nebraska, 1st Nevada and 11th Ohio. Makers mark "Joslyn Firearms Co, Stonington, Conn." on the lockplate.

JOSLYN MODEL 1862 AND 1864 CARBINES	
TYPE:	SINGLE-SHOT CARTRIDGE CARBINE
ORIGIN:	JOSLYN FIREARMS CO., STONINGTON, CONNECTICUT
CALIBER:	.52 RIMFIRE
BARREL LENGTH:	22 INCHES

Below: We show three fine examples of the Joslyn Carbine.

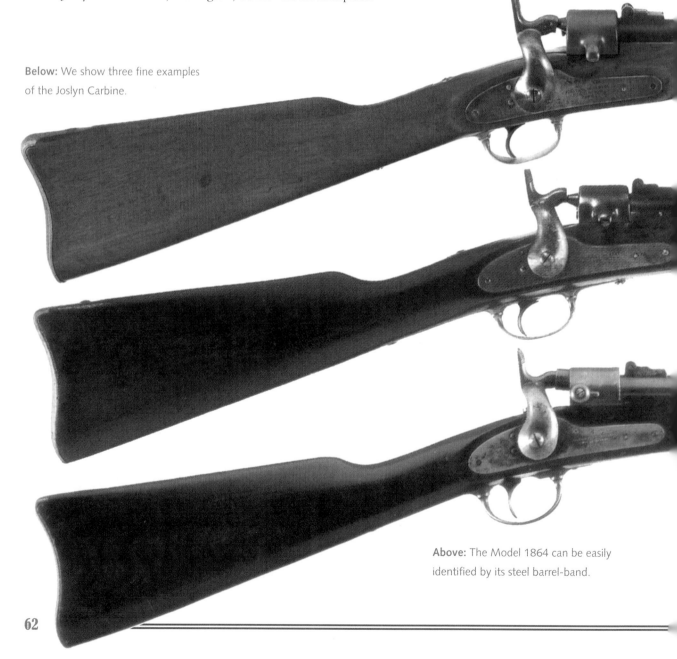

Above: The Model 1864 can be easily identified by its steel barrel-band.

The Model 1862 accounted for about 3,500 of the total run of 16,500 and mainly differs in the style of the latch for the breechblock and an exposed firing pin extension. The later 1864 Model accounts for the bulk of the production, of which some 8,000 units were official Federal government purchases and 4,500 privately purchased through military outfitters like Schuyler, Hartley & Graham in New York.

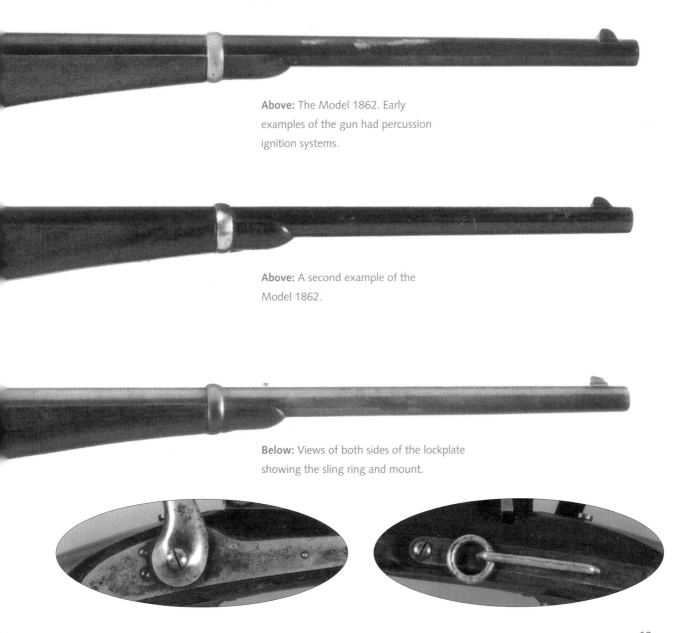

Above: The Model 1862. Early examples of the gun had percussion ignition systems.

Above: A second example of the Model 1862.

Below: Views of both sides of the lockplate showing the sling ring and mount.

Robinson Sharps Carbine

Made in Richmond, Virginia between 1862 and 1864 and based on the Hartford-made Model 1859 Sharps, this weapon generally lacked the refinement and quality workmanship of the original. Approximately 1,900 First Type guns were produced by Robinsons between 1862 and 1863. The Confederate Government took over the Robinson factory in March 1863 and introduced the Second Type, which was identical to the First except for the markings on the breech ("Richmond, VA.").

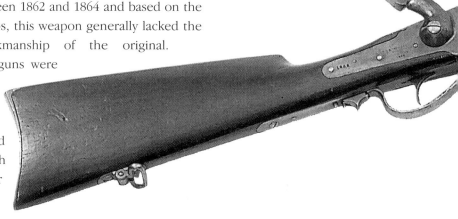

Sharps 1852 Saddle Ring Carbine

After working for other manufacturers, including John Hall at Harpers Ferry, Christian Sharps eventually set up his own company in 1851, in cooperation with Robbins and Lawrence, in Windsor, Vermont. Robbins and Lawrence made the weapons, while Sharps provided technical advice and marketed them from the Sharps Rifle Manufacturing Company, in Hartford, Connecticut. Sharps developed a range of single-shot breech-loading rifles and carbines that were to be heavily used by soldiers in the Civil War and after, and also by sportsmen and hunters.

This is one of Sharps' earlier designs, and is a neat .52 caliber cavalry carbine which used the Sharps patent pellet primer mounted on the lockplate. It is recognizable from later models by the "slanting breech" on the side of the frame. The sling ring bar is unusual in that it extends from the breech to the barrel band. This often seems to have been repaired on surviving examples and perhaps the extra length subjected the part to stress. Some 5,000 units were manufactured in serial numbers 2,050 to 7,500. Our two examples are early guns, being numbered in the 2600 to 3950 range.

Above: The Model 1852 can be identified by its slanting breech.

Above: The S.C. Robinson copy of the Model 1859 Sharps is generally regarded as being inferior to the original in every way.

ROBINSON SHARPS CARBINE

TYPE: PERCUSSION BREECHLOADING CARBINE

ORIGIN: RICHMOND, VIRGINIA

CALIBER: .52

BARREL LENGTH: 21 INCHES

Above: Other distinguishing features are the sling swivel, which is attached to the underside of the buttstock, and the deleted patchbox.

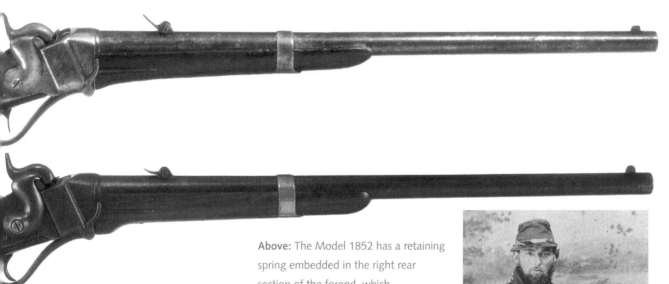

Above: The Model 1852 has a retaining spring embedded in the right rear section of the forend, which disappeared on later models.

SHARPS 1852 SADDLE RING CARBINE

TYPE: PERCUSSION BREECHLOADING CARBINE

ORIGIN: RICHMOND, VIRGINIA

CALIBER: .52

BARREL LENGTH: 21 INCHES

Right: A Union cavalryman poses with his treasured Sharps Carbine resting safely on the table.

Sharps New Model Carbines

As a result of experience with the Model 1852, the Sharps Company updated the design to what is known as the straight breech, or New Model, rifles and carbines. Sharps manufactured 98,000 carbines in Models 1859, 1863, and 1865, although they can be regarded as a single type. The Model 1863, which we are illustrating, was produced both with and without a patchbox (twice as many were made without the patchbox). Both of these examples are without the patchbox..

The Sharps pellet priming system is now integral with the lockplate, the furniture is now iron including the cast barrel band, and the sling ring bar on the left side of the receiver is shorter, extending rearwards to the middle of the wrist. Most of the output was put in the hands of federal troops, but the state of Georgia managed to acquire 2,000 for its cavalry and infantry from the first production of the 1859 model. This was the only batch to retain brass furniture. Ironically, by the time these successful weapons had been developed, Christian Sharps had severed all association with the company, and by 1854 he had formed a new partnership with William Hankins.

Above: Many fine Sharps carbines have survived in excellent condition.

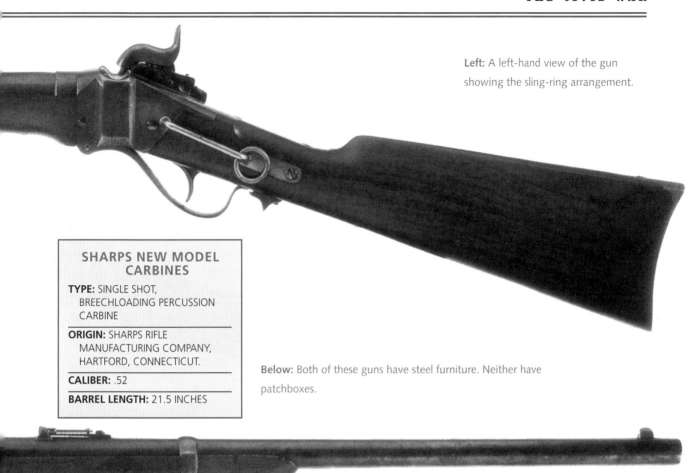

Left: A left-hand view of the gun showing the sling-ring arrangement.

SHARPS NEW MODEL CARBINES

TYPE: SINGLE SHOT, BREECHLOADING PERCUSSION CARBINE

ORIGIN: SHARPS RIFLE MANUFACTURING COMPANY, HARTFORD, CONNECTICUT.

CALIBER: .52

BARREL LENGTH: 21.5 INCHES

Below: Both of these guns have steel furniture. Neither have patchboxes.

Below: Close-ups of both the inspector's cartouche and the upright breech that characterizes later carbines.

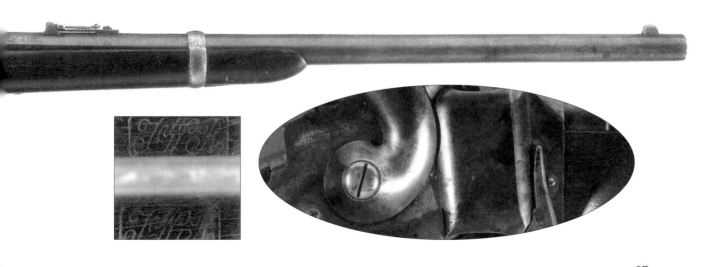

Spencer Repeating Carbine

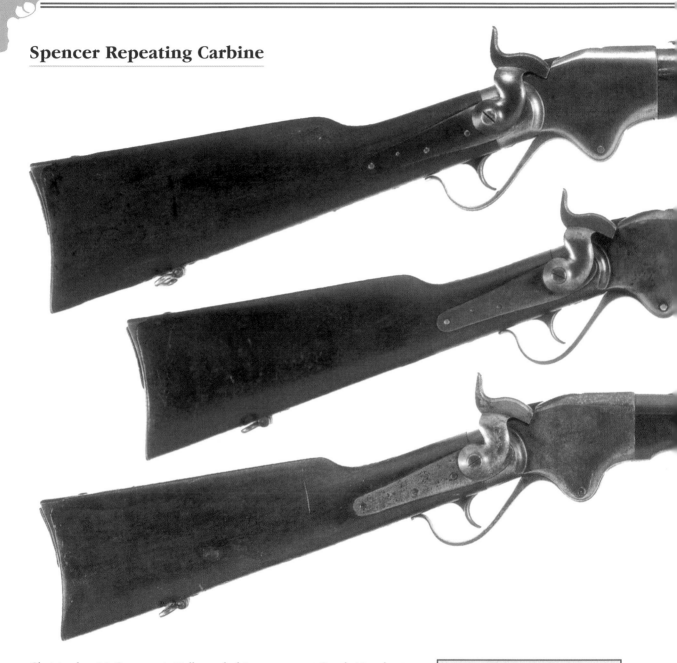

Christopher M. Spencer initially made his weapons at South Manchester, Connecticut, until moving to Boston in about 1862. By that time he had already designed a successful repeating rifle and carbine, the latter of which is described here. This gun was definitely one of the most charismatic, successful and instantly recognizable weapons of the Civil War, and was so well received that it was personally endorsed by President Lincoln after he witnessed a field trial.

The gun is loaded via a tubular magazine housed in the buttstock and rounds are fed into the breech by cranking down the trigger guard lever.

SPENCER REPEATING CARBINE	
TYPE: MAGAZINE-FED REPEATING CARBINE	
ORIGIN: SPENCER REPEATING RIFLE CO., BOSTON, MASSACHUSETTS	
CALIBER: .56-56	
BARREL LENGTH: 22 INCHES	

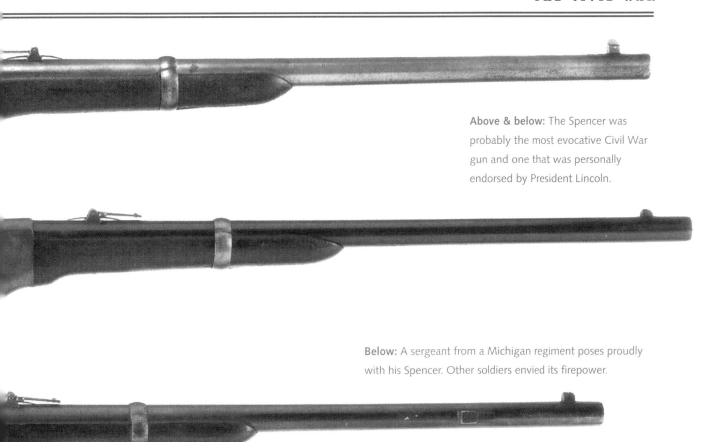

Above & below: The Spencer was probably the most evocative Civil War gun and one that was personally endorsed by President Lincoln.

Below: A sergeant from a Michigan regiment poses proudly with his Spencer. Other soldiers envied its firepower.

Many soldiers were also equipped with the Blakeslee Cartridge Box, a wooden box containing between six and thirteen metal tubes pre-loaded with seven rounds. By placing the end of the reloading tube against the open end of the tubular magazine and dropping the cartridges through, the carbine could be reloaded in a matter of seconds.

The Spencer fired a .52 caliber rimfire straight copper cartridge. The case was actually .56 inches in diameter, so the cartridge is often referred to as the No. 56 or the .56-56.

Several original examples of the 1860 and 1861 models are illustrated. In an age when many of the troops on the Confederate side still carried muzzleloaders, consider the advantages of being issued with a seven-shot repeating weapon. One Confederate soldier captured at Gettysburg by Custer's Spencer-armed 5th Michigan Cavalry exclaimed, "[Spencers] load in the morning and fire all day."

Spencer Model 1865 Carbine

Spencer also produced a later Model 1865, chambered for a .50 cartridge and with a slightly shorter 20-inch barrel. Many were also fitted with the Stabler cut-off, a device which blocked the magazine. If carefully aimed fire was needed, the user could block the magazine and feed single cartridges into the breech, one at a time. The magazine could thus be kept full until rapid fire was needed, whereupon the firer simply slid the cut-off aside and let loose. Spencers continued to be used in the Indian Wars and on the frontier for many years after the Civil War.

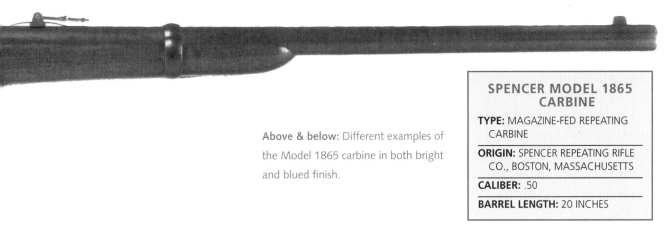

Above & below: Different examples of the Model 1865 carbine in both bright and blued finish.

SPENCER MODEL 1865 CARBINE	
TYPE: MAGAZINE-FED REPEATING CARBINE	
ORIGIN: SPENCER REPEATING RIFLE CO., BOSTON, MASSACHUSETTS	
CALIBER: .50	
BARREL LENGTH: 20 INCHES	

Below: This gun has the addition of a sling swivel on the forend band, a feature more commonly seen on the rifle version.

Right: The trigger guard fits neatly into the stock, showing how well these guns were made. The screw looks like it just left the factory. This is a highly collectible weapon.

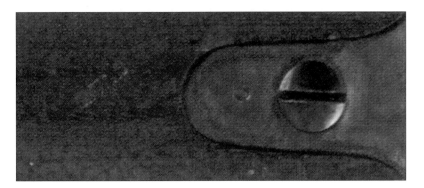

RIFLES

Henry Rifle

Invented and patented by B. Tyler Henry (1821–1898), the Model 1860 was chambered for the .44 Henry cartridge and had a fifteen-round, tubular magazine under the barrel. It had an octagonal 24-inch barrel with no foregrip, but with a walnut buttstock and a brass buttplate. Fourteen thousand of these rifles were made between 1861 and 1866, of which the early examples had iron frames. The remainder, as seen here, had brass frames. When the ring trigger was pushed forward the rearmost round in the magazine was forced into a scoop-shaped carrier by the magazine spring. The hammer was then cocked and the ring trigger drawn to the rear. This lifted the round into the chamber.

The Henry rifle represented some significant advances, the most important being that the sixteen-round magazine gave the shooter a major increase in firepower. It also, however, suffered from some drawbacks, several of which had tactical implications. The first was

HENRY RIFLE
TYPE: TUBULAR-MAGAZINE, LEVER-ACTION RIFLE
ORIGIN: NEW HAVEN ARMS CO., NEW HAVEN, CONNECTICUT
CALIBER: .44 HENRY
BARREL LENGTH: 24.25 INCHES

Above: This particular weapon, with serial number 8794, has been identified as one of a batch of Henrys issued to troops on guard duties in the area of Washington D.C., in the latter part of the Civil War.

Top: Another brass frame Henry, the rifle below carries the serial number 788. The detail shows how a previous owner has fitted his own rearsight into a slot cut into the barrel, which has been made from an "Indian head" penny.

that the shooter's forehand held the barrel, which became very hot in a prolonged engagement. The second, and more important, was that the tubular magazine had to be disengaged and reloaded from the front, which meant that the weapon had to be taken out of action and engage the shooter's attention until the task had been completed. Thirdly, the magazine had slots, which allowed dirt to enter.

The company changed its name from the New Haven Arms Company to the Henry Repeating Rifle Company in 1865 and to the Winchester Repeating Arms Company in 1866. This meant that when these problems were overcome in a new model that was introduced that year, it carried the now legendary name of the "Winchester Model 1866."

Following pages Company A, 7th Illinois Color Guard, were tasked with defending Washington from Confederate attack. They were equipped with the fast-firing Henry rifle.

HIRAM BERDAN AND HIS DISTINGUISHED SHARPSHOOTERS

Above: Hiram Berdan in military uniform. Although he received several brevets, finally attaining the honorary rank of Major General, his practical level of command remained as Colonel.

Right top: An 1861 poster from Windham County, Vermont, challenging recruits to test their skills as Sharpshooters.

Right: A closeup of the famous Sharps action and an original pack of ammunition.

At the outbreak of the Civil War, Hiram Berdan (September 6, 1824–March 31, 1893) was a mechanical engineer living in New York City. He had a special interest in weapons and is reputed to have invented a repeating rifle and a patented musket ball. His inventions include the specially adapted 1859 Berdan Sharps bolt-action rifle, which was to be so valuable in Union service during the war. Berdan was also a crack rifleman and had been the top amateur marksman in the United States since 1846. Always a great self-promoter, Berdan wrote to Secretary of War Edwin M. Stanton, suggesting the establishment of a corps of specially picked marksman to fight on the side of the Union. They were to be equipped with the best possible rifles, making them invaluable as sharpshooters and skirmishers. Stanton agreed the proposal and commissioned Berdan Colonel of the 1st Regiment on November 30, 1861. The marksmen were to be known as Berdan's Sharpshooters. Volunteers were advertised for this "distinguished branch of the service too well known for any comments" and were also invited to examine the "Improved Sharp's hair trigger breech-loading rifle" with which they were to be equipped. Each applicant had to pass a shooting test, and had to put ten bullets in succession within a ten-inch circle at 200 yards at rest and 100 yards off hand, without the benefit of a telescopic sight. During the summer and fall of 1861, eighteen companies of United States Sharpshooters were recruited from eight states and were formed into two regiments. Bounties were paid to enlisting men, $402 to veteran volunteers, and $302 to "all others."

The original recruits were also encouraged to bring their own target rifles and were promised that the government would pay $60 for every suitable rifle, but this promise was never kept. Despite the reservations of the ordnance department and Lincoln's cost concerns, the regiments were ultimately armed with Sharps breech-loading rifles. Although General Scott felt that the weapons would "spoil Berdan's command,"

and Lincoln was worried by the gun's price tag ($35 as opposed to $12 for a Springfield), their issue was finally approved when the Colt revolving rifle proved inadequate.

The 1st Regiment was formed from ten companies, A–K: four from New York, three from Michigan, one from New Hampshire, one from Vermont, and one from Wisconsin. Each company had a commanding captain. The 2nd Regiment had only eight companies, A–H: two from New Hampshire, two from Vermont, one from Minnesota, one from Michigan, one from Pennsylvania, and one from Maine. From September 1891 to March 1862, the chosen recruits were billeted at the U.S.S.S.

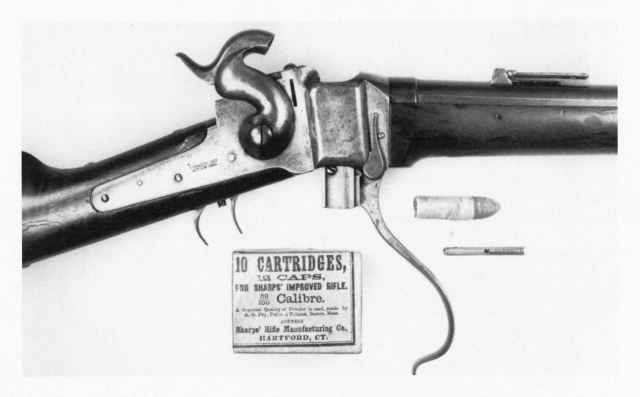

10 CARTRIDGES,
12 CAPS,
FOR SHARPS' IMPROVED RIFLE.
52/100 Calibre.
A Superior Quality of Powder is used, made by A. G. Fay, Potter & Tolman, Boston, Mass.
ADDRESS
Sharps' Rifle Manufacturing Co.,
HARTFORD, CT.

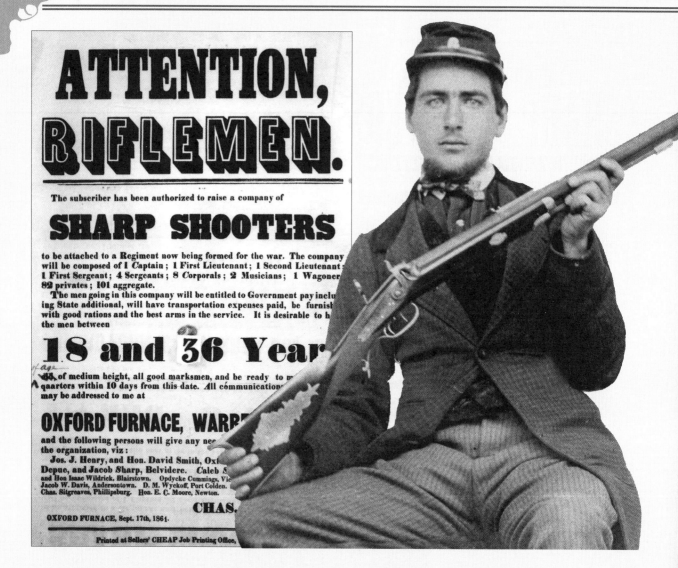

ATTENTION, RIFLEMEN.

The subscriber has been authorized to raise a company of

SHARP SHOOTERS

to be attached to a Regiment now being formed for the war. The company will be composed of 1 Captain ; 1 First Lieutenant ; 1 Second Lieutenant ; 1 First Sergeant ; 4 Sergeants ; 8 Corporals ; 2 Musicians ; 1 Wagoner ; 82 privates ; 101 aggregate.

The men going in this company will be entitled to Government pay including State additional, will have transportation expenses paid, be furnished with good rations and the best arms in the service. It is desirable to h the men between

18 and 36 Year of age

of medium height, all good marksmen, and be ready to r quarters within 10 days from this date. All communication may be addressed to me at

OXFORD FURNACE, WARR

and the following persons will give any ne the organization, viz :

Jos. J. Henry, and Hon. David Smith, Oxf Depue, and Jacob Sharp, Belvidere. Caleb and Hon Isaac Wildrick, Blairstown. Opdycke Cummings, Vic Jacob W. Davis, Andersontown. D. M. Wyckoff, Port Colden. Chas. Sitgreaves, Phillipsburg. Hon. E. C. Moore, Newton.

CHAS.

OXFORD FURNACE, Sept. 17th, 1861.

Printed at Sellers' CHEAP Job Printing Office,

(United States Sharpshooters) Camp of Instruction, which was situated north of Washington. Their tough training revolved around learning how to shoot effectively and economically and to use cover as effectively as possible. All orders were given by bugle call.

The Sharpshooters' uniforms were highly distinctive. Their coats were made from a fine, dark green cloth, as were their black-plumed caps. Originally, their trousers were light blue, but these were later exchanged for green ones. They also had leather leggings and hair-covered calfskin knapsacks that had a cooking kit attached to each one. Unsurprisingly, the Sharpshooters became known as the "Green Coats," and were considered to make a "handsome appearance." A New York Post correspondent said that the regiments reminded him of Robin Hood's outlaws.

Above left: A recruitment poster for Sharpshooter regiments promising "the best arms in the service."

Above right: In the early days of the regiment many recruits brought their own guns as shown here.

Right: Don Troiani's painting of a U.S. Sharpshooter accurately records fine details of his uniform and equipment.

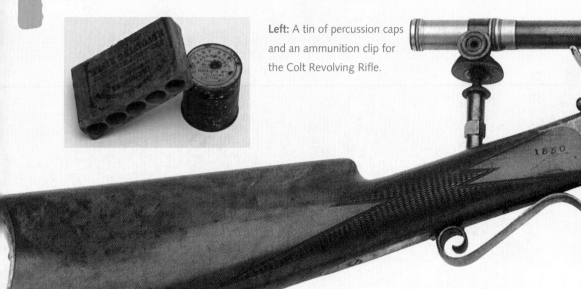

Left: A tin of percussion caps and an ammunition clip for the Colt Revolving Rifle.

Above: The Colt Revolving Rifle Model 1855 with an advanced telescopic sight.

As well as the distinctive uniform, each Sharpshooter was also issued with the following equipment: rifle, bayonet and scabbard, screwdriver, cleaning thong and brush, leather sling, leather cartridge carrier, and leather cap pouch.

The U.S.S.S.'s first skirmish took place against enemy foragers at Lewinsville, Virginia in September 1861, and they ultimately took part in over sixty-five famous battles and actions. These included the advance on Yorktown, Virginia, the Battle of Williamsburg, the Battle of Antietam, the pursuit of Lee to Manassas Gap, Virginia, the Siege of Petersburg, Virginia, the Battle of Fredericksburg, and the "Mud March." The fact that Sharpshooters were normally deployed close to enemy positions meant that they suffered heavy losses during the war (a total of 532 men to wounding and disease), and very few Sharpshooters became prisoners of war. Despite this, their morale was generally very high. Their dangerous and heroic work generated many legends and heroes, including the dead shot "California Joe," and Lorenzo Barber, "the fighting parson." The 1st and 2nd Regiments of Sharpshooters claimed to have killed more Confederates than any other two

Below: Tough training encouraged the Sharpshooters to seek inventive positions to fire on the enemy. Even so, their aggressive stance often exposed them to heavy losses.

regiments on the Union side.

Shortly after the outbreak of war, Berdan was breveted Brigadier General, United States Volunteers at Chancellorsville and was further promoted to Major General, United States Volunteers, for services rendered at the Battle of Gettysburg. This included a scout that he commanded personally on the second day of the battle. But in reality, these brevets were honorary and did not entitle him to command above the level of Colonel.

As time went by, Berdan became an increasingly controversial figure, too involved in the relative superiorities of various rifles, and in pursuing government contracts for his inventions. Indeed, it was said of him that he was more often seen in a parlor than a rifle pit. Both military and

Below: In one of the most famous images of the Sharpshooters, Private Truman Head, nicknamed "California Joe," takes cover behind a convenient rock, Sharps at the ready.

Below: The New Model 1859 Sharps rifle, like this one, was modified with an extra "set" trigger by the Sharpshooters.

Below: An unknown Sharpshooter showing his later issue Sharps rifle and distinctive leather leggings worn over green trousers

civilian contemporaries became antagonistic towards him, believing him to be self-interested, unscrupulous, and unfit for command. His own men became highly critical of his personal ambition and unseemly avoidance of the enemy at all costs—allegations of cowardice, in fact. Day-to-day command of the Sharpshooters was substantially devolved onto the shoulders of Lt. Col. Frederick Mears. Berdan ultimately resigned his commission on January 2, 1864 to pursue his other interests. He went on to develop a twin-screw submarine gunboat, a torpedo boat for evading torpedo nets, a long-distance range finder, and a distance fuze for shrapnel.

Berdan died in 1893 and was buried in Section 2 of Arlington National Cemetery.

The Colt 5-shot revolving rifle

Berdan's Sharpshooters were undoubtedly the most famous Civil War unit to be equipped with the Colt revolving rifle, as Berdan was always at the forefront of equipping his men with more advanced armaments than the standard army issue. Supported by President Lincoln, he received 1,000 Colts from the Ordnance Department. However, the weapons were not as successful as had been anticipated, and were soon replaced with the Sharps. In fact, although Colt had been one of the first arms manufacturers to anticipate that the market for revolving rifles would ultimately be more important than that for pistols, his Model 1855 Military Rifle (in .44 and .56 caliber), and his Model 1855 Revolving Carbine were jointly responsible for only 13,700 units manufactured during the Civil War. This was just a tiny fraction of the weapons required by the Northern forces.

The short sighted Ordnance Department was somewhat to blame for this limited introduction of the Colt, as they were less than enthusiastic about repeating rifles. But the real problem for the gun was that the Spencer and Henry equivalents were actually better and more reliable systems. Colt's Civil War rifle production was therefore concentrated on single-shot .58 caliber rifle muskets (of the type adopted by the Springfield Armory). Springfield contracted out and produced over 500,000 examples of this weapon, while Colt delivered 75,000 units.

Berdan's regiments of Sharpshooters reluctantly accepted the Colts on the basis that these would be replaced by Sharps as soon as they became available. The Colt had a distressing tendency to discharge all of its cylinders at once, which led to some horrific injuries to their users, and they were gladly handed in when the Sharps were introduced in 1862.

Above: A Sharpshooter with a Colt Revolving Rifle. The weapon turned out to be disliked by the men.

Left: Poster from Utica, New York, extolling the virtues of Berdan's improved Sharps rifle, and the green Sharpshooters' uniform.

The Sharps Model 1859 Rifle for Berdan's Sharpshooters

Berdan had always intended that his men should beequipped with Sharps rifles (named after their creator, Christian Sharps), and he cooperated with the company to make several valuable modifications to the gun, without permission from the ordnance department. These included the introduction of the angular bayonet (which made the bayonet lug redundant), the modification of the rear sight to improve long-distance accuracy (at up to 1,000 yards), and the replacement of the single trigger with the double-set trigger (borrowed from the Sharps sporting rifles).

The initial order for 2,000 guns (supplied at $42.50 each, including bayonets) was delivered to the grateful Sharpshooters in 1862. The Sharps were delivered to the 1st Regiment in May, and to the 2nd in June. The guns carried the serial numbers 54374 to 57567, but this range also includes around 1,300 Sharps M1859 carbines and a number of single trigger non-Berdan M1859 rifles. The guns were light (at eight pounds, twelve ounces), compact (47 inches long overall), accurate, and rapid (capable of up to nine rounds per minute). They gave their users immediate satisfaction and were highly valued by the Sharpshooters, becoming known as their "truthful Sharps." The weapon used a .52 caliber conical lead ball, with skin or linen cartridges (containing sixty-four grains of black powder), and was equipped to use Lawrence Pellet primers. The men themselves often preferred the original "hat" percussion caps. As a breechloader, the firearm was capable of being loaded in the prone position, which was ideal for the Sharpshooters. Each man carried forty rounds in his ammunition box and twenty more in his knapsack. One hundred rounds were issued when action was imminent.

Although Berdan came under a hail of criticism from his own men for military incompetence and alleged cowardice, it was his business and political connections that made the issue of Sharps guns to the Sharpshooters possible—weapons that they made the most of and came to value so highly.

Above: Private John Page of Company F, 1st U.S. Sharpshooters with his Sharps at the ready.

Right: Two Sharpshooters, depicted by Don Troiani, showing a variety of different clothing and equipment including the Colt Revolving Rifles that they were originally issued with.

A HISTORY OF SMITH & WESSON

Above: An early Volcanic Army type with a steel frame and an 8-inch barrel in .41 caliber.

Horace Smith and Daniel Wesson formed their first commercial partnership in 1852. The aim of their company was to produce a repeating pistol in which self-contained .40 caliber cartridges were stored in a tubular magazine and chambered using a manual operated lever. This lever doubled as the trigger guard. The firer moved this lever down and forward to extract the used cartridge case and push a new round up and behind the chamber. Pulling the lever backwards chambered the round and re-cocked the action. Smith & Wesson's pistol was available with 6-, 8-, or 16-inch barrels. The example shown at the top is the 8-inch version, which is clearly marked "SMITH & WESSON, NORWICH. CT." The young company lasted for only two years as financial difficulties caused it to fall under the majority ownership of investor Oliver Winchester. The other pictured example is a later version of the gun which was produced by the New Haven Arms Company. This company was to become Winchester.

After the demise of their first company the partners began a new enterprise and in 1856 they opened a new factory in Springfield, Massachusetts. This was a traditional armory town with a skilled labor force.

The aim of the new company was to manufacture a newly designed

revolver and cartridge combination which would become known as the Smith & Wesson Model 1. This gun was based around the Rollin White principle of a bored–through cylinder (the idea that was rejected by Colt) combined with a revolutionary Smith & Wesson-designed metallic cartridge. Smith & Wesson negotiated with Rollin White for assignment of his patent, and agreed to pay him a twenty-five percent royalty on every pistol sold. This gave Smith & Wesson a ten-year head start as

Below: The Smith & Wesson plant in Stockbridge Street, Springfield, Massachusetts.

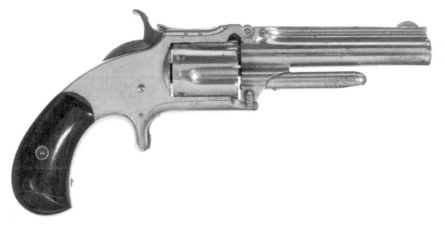

Above: Smith & Wesson Model 1, second issue.

manufacturer of this advanced cartridge loading pistol. The timing of the founding of this new company was fortunate as the looming Civil War provided a perfect market for Smith & Wesson weapons. The partners also developed a larger caliber revolver, the Smith & Wesson Model 2, which was launched in June 1861. This was just two months before the opening shots of the war.

SMITH & WESSON-MODEL 2 ARMY REVOLVER (1861)
TYPE: SIX-ROUND, SERVICE REVOLVER
ORIGIN: SMITH & WESSON, SPRINGFIELD,
MASSACHUSETTS
CALIBER: .32 RIMFIRE
BARREL LENGTH: 3.5INCHES

Above: Smith & Wesson Model 2 Army Revolver (1861)

After the Civil War hostilities ended, the demand for guns slumped to an all–time low. Smith & Wesson began to look overseas for sales opportunities. The company obtained a large order from the Russian military authorities for the Smith & Wesson Model 3. Consequently the gun was nicknamed the "Russian." The model helped to establish the company as one of America's premier firearms makers. The Model 3 was used very widely in the West and was favored by lawman such as Wyatt Earp and outlaws like Jesse James. The United States Army adopted the Model 3. In this context, the gun was called the "Schofield," named after Major George Schofield. Schofield incorporated several design improvements into the gun that were based on his experience of using the gun in the field. As a result the weapon was extremely practical and reliable and was used throughout the Indian Wars of the West.

Smith & Wesson Model 3 Schofield

The Model 3 was a major success for the company and inspired many variations, one of the most interesting being the Schofield Model. Major George Schofield of the U.S. Cavalry liked the Model 3 Smith & Wesson, but patented a number of improvements designed to make it easier to use on horseback and, in particular, to reload while holding the reins. His proposals were accepted and in 1875 a government order for what was now designated the Model 3 Schofield was placed. In essence, Schofield's improvements included a modified barrel catch, improved extraction and a barrel reduced to seven inches. A new round, the .45 Smith & Wesson (which was not interchangeable with the .45 Colt), was also developed for this weapon.

Major Schofield's heavy revolver proved very popular with users, particularly in the cavalry, but by this time the Colt Single-Action Army was so well-established that it stood no chance of long-term adoption and the Army discarded it after some 9,000 had been made. Army stocks were sold off in 1887, some going to National Guard units, some to Wells Fargo

Above: Major George Schofield who made improvements to the Model 3 based on his experience of using the gun in action.

(with barrels shortened to five inches) and the balance to civilian arms dealers, many of which then found their way to the Western frontier. According to historians of the period, Schofields were carried by outlaws such as Frank and Jesse James and Bill Tilghman.

During production there were some minor variations, which have been labeled Schofield First and Second Models, the most visible difference being in the latch. The First Model shown here has a latch with a pointed spur and a washer around the head of the latch retaining screw.

SPECIFICATIONS

TYPE: SIX-ROUND, HINGED-FRAME, SINGLE-ACTION REVOLVER

ORIGIN: SMITH & WESSON, SPRINGFIELD, MASSACHUSETTS

CALIBER: .45 S&W

BARREL LENGTH: 7 INCHES

Left: The Second Model shown here has a large circular device at the head of the latch and no washer surrounding the retaining screw.

Smith & Wesson Model 3 "Russian"

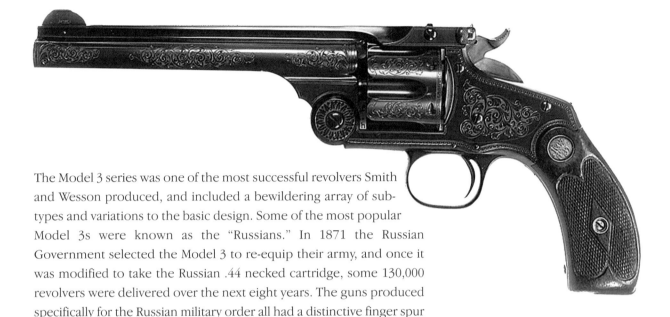

The Model 3 series was one of the most successful revolvers Smith and Wesson produced, and included a bewildering array of sub-types and variations to the basic design. Some of the most popular Model 3s were known as the "Russians." In 1871 the Russian Government selected the Model 3 to re-equip their army, and once it was modified to take the Russian .44 necked cartridge, some 130,000 revolvers were delivered over the next eight years. The guns produced specifically for the Russian military order all had a distinctive finger spur on the trigger guard which was found to be an encumbrance by most American users and many were ground off.

Smith and Wesson also used the Russian cartridge in commercial weapons, and many thousands were sold, both on the U.S. domestic market and to overseas governments. Smith and Wesson "Russians" were adopted in various quantities by Turkey, Japan, Australia, Argentina, Spain, England, and others.

All followed the same basic outline, with the barrel and cylinder tipping forward around a large hinge pin in front of the cylinder. A star ejection system allowed for quick reloading, while a retaining catch locked the weapon closed just in front of the hammer.

The "Russian" shown here was made for the U.S. civilian market, and is a beautifully prepared piece, with extensive engraving on the frame, barrel and cylinder, all offset by gilt inlay. The finely checkered grips are walnut.

**SMITH & WESSON
MODEL 3 "RUSSIAN"**

TYPE: SIX-ROUND, HINGED-
FRAME, SINGLE-ACTION
REVOLVER

ORIGIN: SMITH & WESSON,
SPRINGFIELD,
MASSACHUSETTS

CALIBER: .44 RUSSIAN

BARREL LENGTH: 6 INCHES

Following page: A Russian Cossack wears his Smith & Wesson on a lanyard, using the trigger guard spur to anchor the gun on his belt.

THE INDIAN WARS

From 1865 to 1890, the United States cavalry played a huge role in western expansion, patrolling the frontier and protecting would-be settlers from attack by the native tribes. Effectively, the frontier started west of the Mississippi River, and as western settlement became increasingly widespread, the cavalry became responsible for a huge area of territory. The cavalry also became a major enforcer of the civil law in the region and became involved in many actions to bring lawbreakers and gunmen to justice. A good example of this would be the 1870 shootout between Wild Bill Hickok and riders of the Seventh Cavalry that took place in Hays, Kansas. Hickok killed one cavalry officer and wounded another.

The role of the cavalry in the post-Civil War period was determined in 1869, when President Grant appointed William Tecumseh Sherman

Below: A Model 1851 Colt Navy of the type used by Hickok.

Above: The Colt Single-Action Army revolver was adopted by the United States Cavalry soon after its launch in 1873.

and the Commander General of the United States Army and the cavalry also came under his command. At this time, Sherman's major preoccupation was the subjugation of the Indian tribes, which he saw as a barrier to westward expansion. To this end, he created the Plains Cavalry and recruited an additional four regiments to deal with the so-called "Indian problem." The American Indian Wars raged until the Massacre of Wounded Knee in 1890 and became the focus of the Plains Cavalry for over two decades. Each cavalry regiment consisted of twelve troops of approximately ninety-five men. Recruiting officers into the cavalry was no problem, as many men stayed in the army when the Civil War ended. But it proved much harder to engage ordinary troopers. The ranks became filled with many wanted men and immigrants, not all of whom spoke English.

Cavalry Regiments of the Indian Wars

The 7th United States Cavalry was undoubtedly the most famous regiment to fight in the Indian Wars. Constituted in 1866, the regiment was made up of twelve companies. Like most of the post-war cavalry, its troops were armed mainly with single-action Colt .45 revolvers and modified single-shot .50 caliber Model 1865 Spencer carbines. These were based on the Spencer Model 1863 of the early Civil War era, but had shorter, 20-inch barrels. Beginning in 1874, these guns were finally replaced by the Springfield Model 1873.

Until 1871, the 7th Cavalry Regiment was based at Fort Riley in Kansas. Its mission was to enforce law in the subjugated South. But the regiment was also involved in anti-Native American action, including the famous 1868 Battle of Washita River.

Opposite: Colonel Forsyth's stand at Arikara Fork in 1868 was but one of several fights with the Indians where the army was outnumbered and outgunned. As a result the call for repeating firearms grew louder.

Below: This Indian-made weapon was converted by hand from a Springfield musket. It features a cut-down barrel (21¾ inches from the original forty), a shortened forend. Its barrel band is made from cloth and sinew. The stock is decorated with the characteristic brass tacks.

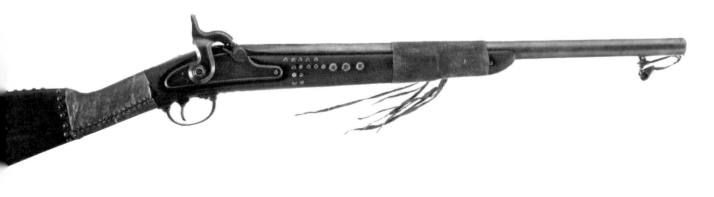

Commanded by General Custer, the 7th Cavalry attacked Chief Black Kettle's Cheyenne village. Even at the time, Custer's attack on a sleeping village was controversial. The General was accused of sadism and his men blamed for killing women and children indiscriminately

In 1873, the 7th United States Cavalry moved to its base to Fort Abraham Lincoln in Dakota Territory. The regiment's initial brief was to reconnoiter and map the Black Hills mountain range that stretches between South Dakota and Wyoming. Custer's discovery of gold in the Black Hills, during his expedition of 1874, had a profound effect on the

Below left: A United States Cavalryman with a Springfield rifle.

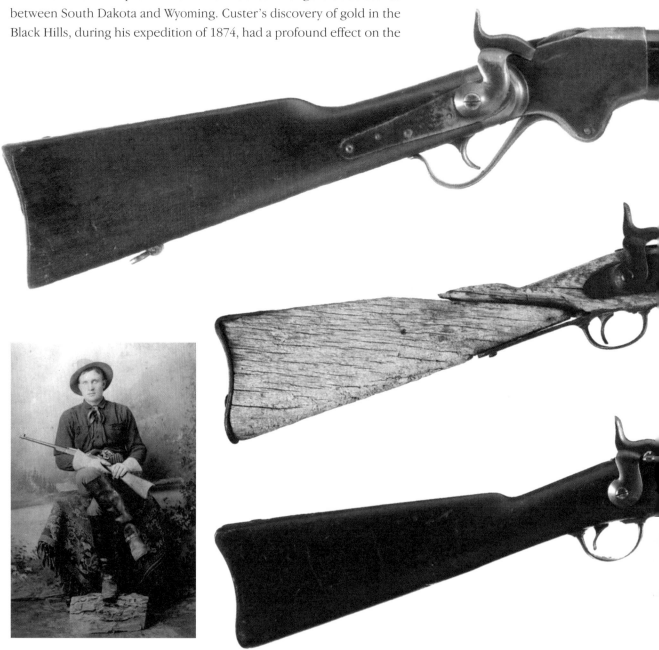

region. Not only did this discovery precipitate the huge social upheaval of the Gold Rush, but it also exacerbated conflict with the Sioux and Lakota tribes, who were under the leadership of Sitting Bull and Crazy Horse. Modern historians accuse President Grant of deliberately provoking war with the Native Americans. Grant was desperate for gold-fuelled growth to lift the economy out of depression.

Above: The Spencer Model 1865 carbine as used by the U.S. Cavalry in the Indian Wars had a shorter 20-inch barrel and was chambered for the .50 cartridge.

Above: This Springfield Model 1873 is thought to have been recovered from the battlefield at Little Bighorn.

Above: This is an early production example of the Springfield Model 1873.

But victory against the Sioux and Cheyenne peoples was only achieved at a huge cost to the men of the 7th Cavalry. The Battle of the Little Big Horn (which took place on June 25 and June 26 1876 and is also known as Custer's Last Stand) saw fifty-two percent of the regiment fall. The final half hour of the engagement resulted in the deaths of 210 cavalrymen. Two hundred and fifty-eight people perished altogether. These included Custer himself, two of his brothers (Captain Thomas Custer, and their youngest brother, civilian scout and forage master, Boston Custer), and the Custer brothers' nephew, Autie Reed.

Below: 1868's Washita Massacre, when Custer's forces attacked a sleeping Indian village, was controversial even at the time.

This rout occurred mainly because of a highly ill-advised decision on the General's part to mount an attack on an Indian village in the Montana Territory. Every man and horse of the 7th Cavalry that fought at Little Big Horn perished at the scene. The single exception was Captain Keogh's famous mount, Comanche. Custer's Last Stand was the most devastating defeat ever suffered by the United States Cavalry.

Above: Custer's favorite gun, a .50 caliber Remington single shot rifle. He wrote to the company to praise the gun.

Below: Custer with his Indian scouts. His favorite Remington rifle is leaning against the guy.

A HISTORY OF WINCHESTER FIREARMS

The origins of the Winchester Repeating Arms Company's success began with the Volcanic Rifle that was originally manufactured by Smith & Wesson. When the company failed in 1856 it was bought out by its main shareholder Oliver Winchester who was convinced that the gun had a viable future. The New Haven Arms Company formed by him in 1857 set to work to improve the gun. Newly recruited plant superintendent Benjamin Tyler Henry was commissioned to improve the cartridge of the Volcanic. Winchester also made the decision to abandon the handgun market and got Henry to concentrate on building a repeating rifle.

Henry's resultant design for a self-contained .44 metallic rim-fire cartridge was combined with a new rifle based on the Volcanic. It used the lever action breech mechanism of the earlier gun and had a tubular magazine. This firearm became the Henry Rifle of 1860. It was used by Union troops in the Civil War and proved to be very effective.

Because of the commercial success of the gun he had improved, Benjamin Tyler Henry felt that he had not been adequately rewarded by Winchester. Eventually, he left the company and as an agent provocateur continued trying to regain control of the gun design he considered to be his.

Above: Benjamin Tyler Henry developed the famous forerunner to the Winchester repeating rifles.

HENRY RIFLE

TYPE: 15-SHOT LEVER ACTION REPEATING RIFLE

CALIBER: .44 RIM-FIRE

BARREL LENGTH: 24¼ INCHES

BARREL SHAPE: HEXAGONAL

STOCK: WALNUT

YEAR OF MANUFACTURE: 1860 TO 1866

QUANTITY MADE: 14,000

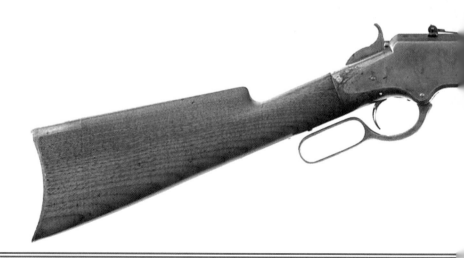

The Winchester Model 1866

After the Civil War ended Winchester moved to Bridgeport, Connecticut and changed the company name to The Winchester Repeating Arms Company. This was to distance the company from any further association with Henry. Oliver Winchester also hired a new superintendent, Nelson King. His role was to improve the slightly aging Henry rifle in order to revive sales in the post-war slump.

The distinctive brass frame of the Henry rifle was to be retained in the new Model 1866 to utilize tooling and brass materials left over from earlier Henry production. King's major improvement was the addition of the loading port on the side of the frame. This enabled the rifle to be loaded without access to the end of the magazine tube and a wooden forestock which made the gun more comfortable to hold. The Henry relied on the shooter gripping the steel magazine tube which, because it was attached to the barrel, became very hot under continuous fire. The shorter barrels of the carbine version made for a much more ergonomic gun. For use on horseback a saddle ring was added to the left side of the rear of the gun frame.

Above: Winchester plant superintendent Nelson King further developed the Henry rifle by adding a loading port to the side of the action. The result was the Model 1866 Winchester.

Above: An iron frame Henry; the majority of the guns had brass frames.

Below: The 1866 Carbine was named the "Yellow Boy" after its distinctive brass receiver.

Right: The familiar slot in the side which received bullets. Normal loading was by thumbing the shells in.

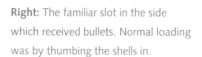

King's improvements were more generously rewarded than those of his predecessor Benjamin Tyler Henry. The company's board of directors voted King a bonus of $5,000. Maybe they had learnt from the debacle with Henry. King's earnings were reputedly the highest in the firm apart from those of Winchester himself. Some 157,000 Winchester Model 1866s were produced between 1866 and 1891. These included 118,000 carbines, 6,000 rifles, and 13,000 muskets.

Above: Photograph of Oliver Fisher Winchester, without his familiar beard.

Right: Winchester rifles were popular with law enforcement groups like these Texas Rangers.

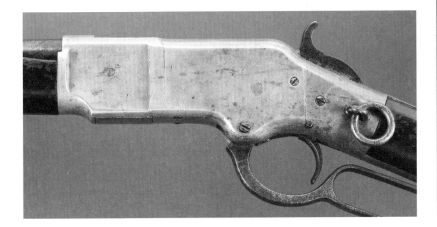

Below: This left-side view shows the carbine ring.
At $40, a cowhand couldn't afford to lose this gun.

1866 CARBINE

CALIBER: 0.44 INCH RIM FIRE CARTRIDGE

LENGTH OF BARREL: 20 INCHES

BARREL SHAPE: ROUND

FINISH: BLUE STEEL BARREL, BRASS FRAME AND RECEIVER

GRIPS: WALNUT

ACTION: UNDER LEVER REPEATING WITH 14 SHOT MAGAZINE

YEAR OF MANUFACTURE: 1866-91

MANUFACTURER: WINCHESTER REPEATING ARMS COMPANY, NEW HAVEN, CONNECTICUT

Right: Patent drawing of the Model 1866 rifle with King's Improvement. Before this improvement, with the Henry rifle, the cartridges had to be loaded from the front of the magazine.

Below: New Haven Arms Co. plant, as seen in 1859. The figure in the window is supposedly Oliver Winchester.

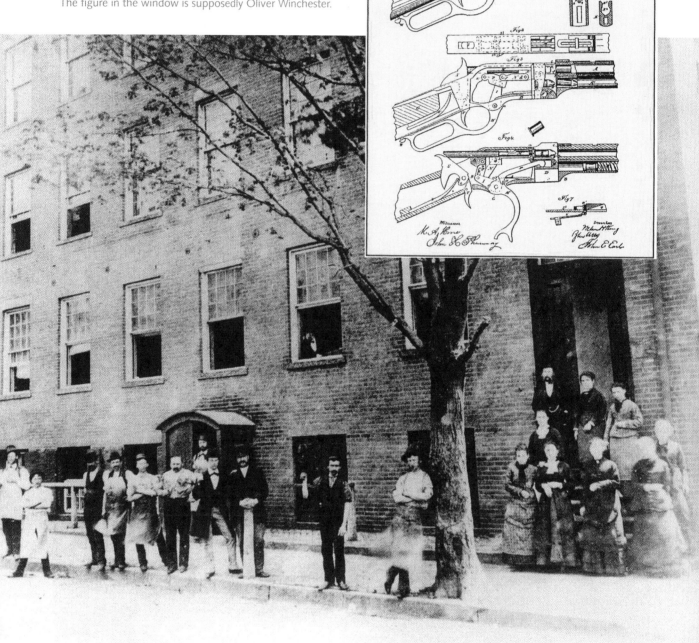

Winchester Model 1873

The Model 1873 offered three advances over the Model 1866. First, it had a stronger frame, which was originally made of iron, but from 1884 of steel. Secondly, it had a dust cover over the action. Thirdly, and perhaps most important of all, however, was that although other calibers were available, most were chambered for the .44-40 round, which was the same as the one used in the Colt single-action revolver, thus greatly easing the user's logistical problems, particularly in the rigorous environment of the frontier. Indeed, the Model 1873 had a thoroughly well-deserved title of "The Gun That Won The West." As with the Model 1866, the Model 1873 was sold in three versions: musket with 30-inch round barrel; sporting rifle with 24-inch round, octagonal, or round/octagonal barrel; and carbine with 20-inch round barrel. There are also the usual minor changes over the production run, mainly concerning the dust-cover. In 1884, Winchester introduced a new version of the Model 1873 chambered for .22 rimfire, but it did not prove particularly popular, with some 19,000 sold over a twenty-year production run. Overall some 720,000 Model 1873s of all versions had been sold when production ended in 1919.

Above: A cowboy proudly displays his Winchester Model 1873.

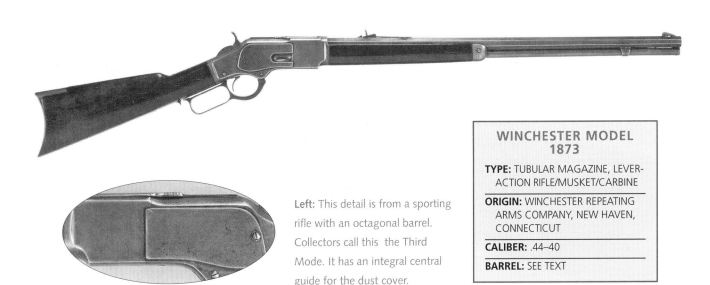

Left: This detail is from a sporting rifle with an octagonal barrel. Collectors call this the Third Mode. It has an integral central guide for the dust cover.

WINCHESTER MODEL 1873	
TYPE:	TUBULAR MAGAZINE, LEVER-ACTION RIFLE/MUSKET/CARBINE
ORIGIN:	WINCHESTER REPEATING ARMS COMPANY, NEW HAVEN, CONNECTICUT
CALIBER:	.44–40
BARREL:	SEE TEXT

OTHER WINCHESTER MODELS

Model 1876

The Model 1876 incorporated changes necessitated by the more powerful cartridges that were coming into use. It had a larger more robust receiver. The sporting rifle version shown here had a 28-inch round barrel together with a correspondingly longer forend.

Model 1885

The Winchester Model 1885 used the first patent that the company bought from John M. Browning. It was the first single-shot rifle to be manufactured by the company. Winchester manufactured 139,000 of these weapons between 1885 and 1920. There were two variants: the "High Wall" and "Low Wall." The difference was defined by the angle of the frame where it covers the hammer. On the Low Wall version, the frame leaves the hammer and breech visible. On the High Wall version, only the spur of the hammer is visible.

Above: A Model 1876 Sporting Rifle with a 28-inch round barrel, chambered for the .45 round.

Above: A standard Winchester Model 1885 High Wall sporting rifle with a 30-inch .38-55 caliber barrel.

Above: An example of the "Low Wall" type where the frame continues forward at the same angle of the top of the wrist thus exposing the hammer and breech.

Model 1894

This gun used the first of the smokeless powder cartridges. Although the days of the traditional West were drawing to a close, working cowboys and villains were still keen to exploit the latest weapons technology. The Wild Bunch was still operating when this gun was released.

Model 1886

The Model 1886 was designed by John Moses Browning. It was designed to handle the more powerful center-fire cartridges that were becoming available. There were three basic configurations of the weapon: rifle, musket, and carbine. The rifle option was available in five different variants, including the sporting, "fancy" sporting, and takedown models. This version is the lightweight model, fitted with a shortened magazine and a cut back forend.

Model 1890

This Winchester model was also designed by the Browning Brothers. It was the company's first ever slide-action rifle. It achieved great popularity, selling over 775,000 units. The gun was a late entry in the story of the West, but was a great little hunting gun for the trail.

Model 1895

John Browning's Model 1895 was the first Winchester lever-action rifle to feature a box magazine. In this case, it was non-detachable, and held five rounds. The gun received the highest possible endorsement when it was adopted by Theodore Roosevelt as his favorite hunting rifle.

Above & left: This is the Model 1886 Lightweight with a half-length magazine and cut-back forearm. It has a 20-inch barrel in .33 WCH caliber.

Left: Members of the Medicine Lodge citizens' posse, with their Winchester rifles.

THE FUR TRAPPERS

Above: The Model 1892 was essentially an updated version of the Model 1873. It employed a slightly smaller version of Browning's improved Model 1886 action, and was available in five different calibers. This is the Trapper's Carbine, which has a 14-inch barrel.

Although the fur trade was largely over by 1840, there remained a rugged body of men who still enjoyed the outdoors existence lived by the original mountain men. They trekked through the mountains and backwoods, sharing camps and sheltered in isolated cabins. These were constructed of logs or lengths of sawn timber supported by a stone fireplace and chimney. Their normal mode of transport was the mule which was hardier than a horse. They usually had dogs for companionship and to help in flushing out game.

Their prey was animals such as the possum, lynx, and beaver whose pelts could still fetch good money. It was still possible to eke out a living by fur trapping rights up to the end of the frontier period.

The trappers' way of life was recognized by gun manufacturers like Winchester and Marlin who both produced specially adapted Trappers Carbines. These guns had short barrels to make them more useable in tight places.

Below: The Marlin Model 1894 version of the Trappers Carbine had a 16-inch barrel.

Below: Trappers and hunters led a very Spartan way of life, sheltering in deserted cabins whenever they could.

THE BUFFALO HUNTERS

Beginning in the early part of the nineteenth century, the Plains were gradually stripped of their herds of buffalo. Early pioneers such as the mountain men killed buffalos to provide food and basic equipment. They did this in the same way that the Native Americans had done to supplement their diet and to provide clothing and shelter.

However, these small inroads into the population of the buffalo herds were nothing compared to the wholesale slaughter that occurred following the Civil War.

Western expansion led many people to hold the view that everything in the region was there to be exploited. As a result of this thinking the mighty buffalo herds were hunted down and slaughtered to virtual extinction. Many of the buffalo hides and meat were shipped back to the meat-hungry East, but an increasing proportion of these products went to sustain life in the growing frontier towns.

To fulfil the market for buffalo products, a breed of professional hunters came into being. These were men who killed these magnificent beasts coolly and scientifically using the modern weapons at their disposal. By the end of the nineteenth century several firearms had been specifically designed for this purpose, weapons with exceptional stopping power. In the early days of the century the only available hunting guns were smoothbore flintlocks. It took a great deal of skill to bring down large game with basic firearms like these.

Typically, the guns that facilitated the slaughter of the buffalo herds were large bore, single-shot weapons such as the Sharps Buffalo Gun. This was a rifle version of the popular Civil War carbine. It was available in .45-70 and .50 caliber and had a choice of 28- or 30-inch barrels. This gun had the necessary stopping power to bring down an animal as big as a buffalo. Other popular choices were the Spencer

Below: Mounds of buffalo hides drying in the sun in Robert Wright's yard in Dodge City, Kansas in 1878.

Sporting Rifle and the Remington Rolling Block big .50 caliber. General Custer used the latter firearm as a hunting gun.

Another nail in the coffin of the buffalo herds was the popularity of shooting at the plains herds from trains. The Kansas Pacific Railroad Company ran special excursions for so-called big game hunters who blasted away at the unsuspecting animals from the comfort and safety of a railroad car. The railroad company even employed its own taxidermist to mount their customers' trophies.

Above: Buffalo hunters at their camp in Texas, 1877.

Following pages: This Currier & Ives print of 1871 shows the Plains being crossed by the new railroad. In the background, buffalo herds run from the fire on the prairie. A few years later there were no buffalos left.

Sharps Model 1874 Sporting Rifle

Sharps rifles were very popular with sporting shooters and hunters and 6,000 of this model were sold. The one above is chambered for .45-70 with a 28-inch octagonal barrel.

Spencer Sports of Buffalo Rifle

(Below) This heavy caliber (up to .56) was popular for shooting big game such as buffalo because of its stopping power. This repeating gun started out as a carbine during the Civil War. It became a popular gun on the frontier. In this case the rifle has been modified by the fitting of a heavy octagonal barrel by gunmaker A.J. Plate of San Francisco.

Remington Rolling Block Sporting Rifle

(Bottom) Remington developed a range of sporting rifles utilizing their successful single-shot rolling block action. The version shown here is fitted with a heavy octagonal barrel in .50 caliber with plain open sights, sporting stock, and forend. Custer himself used one of these guns for big game hunting and wrote to Remington to endorse the weapon.

Above: A Buffalo hunter's kit. It is believed to be the best-preserved and most complete kit to have survived from the days of the frontier.

A HISTORY OF REMINGTON FIREARMS

Eliphalet Remington Sr. was the father of the founder of Remington Arms. He settled in New York's Mohawk River Valley in 1799. His intention was to establish one of the finest forging operations in the frontier. Remington fashioned quality iron implements needed by settlers. These included agricultural tools, household hardware, sleigh runners, and other rudimentary products. As it turned out, Eliphalet's choice of business location paid handsome dividends. Just a few years later in 1824, the Erie Canal was constructed only a few miles to the north of the Mohawk River Valley. The newly constructed waterway provided a direct link to Albany and New York City to the east and to Buffalo and the frontier to the west.

Remington legend states that in 1816, young Eliphalet asked his father for money for a rifle and was refused. Thereupon, so goes the

Below: Another of the original armory buildings built in what would become Ilion, New York, circa 1854.

tale, the young man went out to the smithy and forged and welded a rifle barrel for himself. Putting the barrel on his shoulder Eliphalet walked to Utica to have a gunsmith ream and rifle the barrel. The gunsmith is reported to have praised Eliphalet's work. The lad duly hiked home and finished the rifle—and he was in the gun business! This story has been retold countless times since, but it is unlikely to be true. It is most unlikely that a country boy would have possessed the skills to make up an entire flintlock rifle in 1816. There is little doubt that young Eliphalet did forge his first rifle barrel in that year. After all, he was the son of a commercial iron forger with the facilities of an ironworks at his disposal. To make his barrel, young Eliphalet would have started with a flat iron bar. This would have been around three quarters of an inch thick, about five inches wide, and as long as the finished barrel was to be, so about thirty-six or thirty-nine inches. He would then have heated a short stretch of the bar and forged it lengthwise around a mandrel. A mandrel is a rod used to form and maintain the hollow bore. Bringing the iron to a welding heat he would then have hammered the joint under a trip hammer until it was securely welded together. He would have continued this process, inch by inch, until the whole barrel was welded up and would then have ground the exterior to an octagonal form. At this point, the barrel would have been ready for reaming and rifling. This would have been the customary way to make an iron rifle barrel in the early nineteenth century. But whether Eliphalet finished the rifle after the Utica gunsmith had reamed and rifled the rough barrel is much more questionable.

Above: Two Remington Jenks Navy Rifles. These firearms were nicknamed "mule ears" because of the unusual breech configuration.

Legend has it that Eliphalet's finished rifle was so successful that the Remingtons' neighbors wanted similar rifles for themselves, and he found himself in the gunsmith business. But this is also most unlikely. There is no evidence to indicate that Eliphalet made complete flintlock or percussion sporting or hunting rifles for others until much later on. But it is true that by the mid-1820s, Remington's forge was turning out rifle barrels as well as agricultural tools.

Long before the introduction of the industrial production line, Eliphalet Remington developed a system to organize groups of journeymen into the "inside contracting system." This system organized workers into quality teams who were inspired to innovate and succeed within the framework of Remington.

To satisfy the need for quality gun barrels and later for complete firearms, the sciences of metallurgy and of machine tool technology had to be improved and extended. At this time, Remington introduced the use of cast steel gun barrels.

The Jenks carbines supplied by Remington to the United States Navy in 1848 and 1849 were the first un-welded steel barrels ever used by the American armed forces. New materials dictated new technologies, and Remington designed and built machine tools to drill, ream, rifle, and finish these new solid steel barrels.

Following the Mexican War of the late 1840s, Remington took a commanding lead in fabricating interchangeable parts. This was the forerunner of modern industrial mass-production. The so-called American system of manufacturing owed a lot to Remington's foresight. The system was introduced in 1845 and became the standard method of manufacture throughout the world. It relies on semi-skilled labor to assemble interchangeable parts with the use of machine tools and jigs. Remington understood the importance of the interrelationship of component parts and the tolerance levels necessary to achieve true interchangeability. Remington was one of the first to combine the concept of interchangeable parts with progressive assembly methods. His application of the American system put Remington Arms in an enviable position by the time of the Civil War. Government orders placed during the war led to an unprecedented expansion of Remington's plant, personnel, and production. Upwards of a thousand workers were employed in the company's armories at Ilion and in nearby Utica. These facilities reached a peak production of 200 pistols and over 1,000 rifles a day. In all, E. Remington and Sons supplied 40,000 muskets, 12,500 rifles, more than 144,000 revolvers, and 20,000 Remington carbines to the United States Army and Navy during the Civil

Above: Remington Custom shop workers around 1890. Shop superintendent L.N. Walker stands in the center of the back row.

War. (The carbines were subcontracted to the Savage Revolving Rifle
Company.)

Remington was also preeminent in the field of ammunition design
and manufacture. The company manufactured pistol, rifle, and shotgun
ammunition from 1871 until 1885. In 1888, the assets of E. Remington
& Sons were taken over by Schuyler, Hartley, & Graham, a New York

City arms dealer that also controlled the Union Metallic Cartridge Company of Bridgeport, Connecticut. Union Metallic had been in operation since 1866. Marcellus Hartley took control of both companies, and through his leadership the business seized a commanding position in the field of small arms ammunition, a position that it has held ever since.

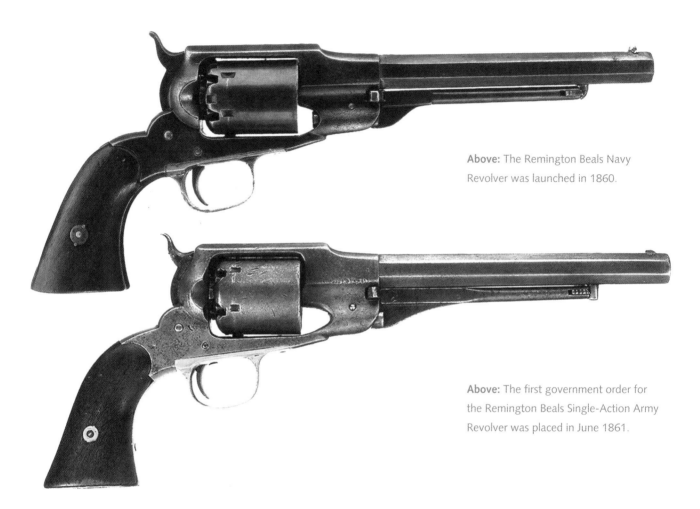

Above: The Remington Beals Navy Revolver was launched in 1860.

Above: The first government order for the Remington Beals Single-Action Army Revolver was placed in June 1861.

Remington Rolling Block Rifles, Pistols and Carbines

Joseph Rider developed the Remington split-breech system during the Civil War, and adapted it to both small-frame and large-frame carbines. At the same time he continued to experiment with various methods of locking the breech and on December 16, 1864 Rider submitted a new breech design to the patent office. On January 3, 1865 Rider received the first patent for what would evolve into the famous Remington rolling block action. The rolling block system refers to a breech system comprised of a hammer piece that is brought to cocking position, and a semi-circular breechblock that is rotated back to open the breech. The spent shell casing can then be extracted and a new cartridge inserted into the breech.

Remington knew that Rider's rolling block action breech loading system was a winning design. The company encouraged Rider's developments and sought to interest Ordnance department officials in their new design. Remington finally received the news that they and the other gun manufacturers had been waiting for. An Ordnance Board was to convene in Washington, D.C., in March 1866 to determine the best possible breech loading rifle and carbine for use by the United States Army. Remington knew that if the United States Army adopted a Remington System, it would be the solution to their immediate cash flow problems and the relative inactivity of their armory.

The Navy Bureau of Ordnance was firmly convinced of the merits of the Remington rolling block system. So they decided to order Remington rolling blocks carbines for shipboard service. On October 22, 1867 Remington signed the contract to fabricate 5,000 Remington Model 1867 Rolling Block Navy Carbines. These guns were delivered to the United States Navy between July 1868 and February 1869.

Below: Chief Touch-The-Clouds poses with what is thought to be Custer's favorite rifle plundered from the battlefield at Little Big Horn.

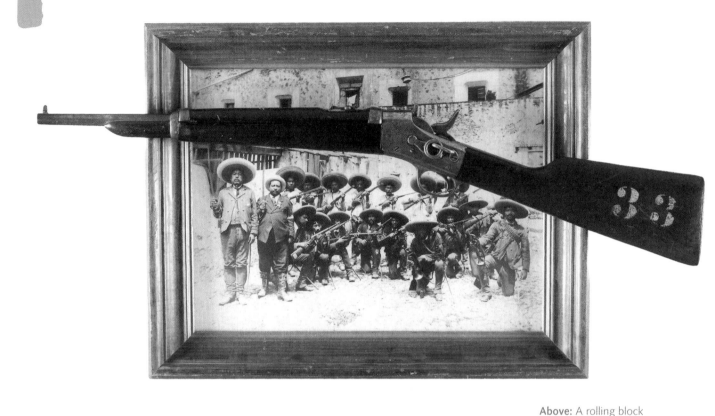

Above: A rolling block carbine in front of a photograph of the Mexican "Rurales" who are armed with the gun.

Sadly, Remington never did get the big army contract for long arms. The United States Army ordered Springfield carbines instead. This was largely for economic reasons. Most of Remington's success during the frontier period was derived from the American civilian market and orders from overseas military forces. Between 1869 and 1873 the Republic of Mexico acquired an assortment of 6,268 Remington rifles, carbines, and revolvers. It is believed that a number of these were rolling block conversions where muskets were adapted to breechloaders. In 1874 Mexico purchased 10,000 Remington Mexican Model 1871 Rolling Block Rifles. These guns were said to be the first modern firearms ordered for its poorly armed military forces. Later in the same year Mexico ordered another 40,000 Remington rifles and carbines.

Above The Remington 1890 New Model Army revolver was the final development in the company's revolver range but was overshadowed by more popular guns like Colt's Single Action Army.

Remington Model 1871 Army Pistol

Remington won a government contract which led to the supply of the Model 1871 Army pistol; a number were also made for the civilian market. The two examples shown here illustrate the difference between a standard model and a custom-built, fully decorated "de luxe" example. The standard model has a case-hardened (blue) finish, with walnut grips, with the inspector's cartouche clearly visible on the left side of the grip. The weapon has obviously been used during its 140-year life, but remains a thoroughly serviceable and handsome example of the gunsmith's skill.

REMINGTON MODEL 1871 ARMY PISTOL
TYPE: SINGLE-SHOT, ROLLING-BLOCK PISTOL
ORIGIN: REMINGTON ARMS CO., INC., ILION, NEW YORK.
CALIBER: .50 CENTERFIRE
BARREL LENGTH: 8 INCHES

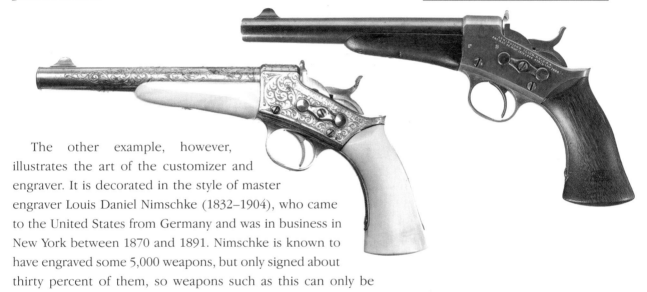

The other example, however, illustrates the art of the customizer and engraver. It is decorated in the style of master engraver Louis Daniel Nimschke (1832–1904), who came to the United States from Germany and was in business in New York between 1870 and 1891. Nimschke is known to have engraved some 5,000 weapons, but only signed about thirty percent of them, so weapons such as this can only be described as "Nimschke-style." The scroll-work is exceptionally detailed and the pistol is set off by the flawless ivory stocks.

Above: The Remington rolling block single-shot pistol was popular with target shooters.

Remington Model 1890 New Model Army Revolvers

In 1891, the Remington Arms Company introduced the Remington Model 1890 New Model Army revolver. This was a six-shot handgun in 44-40 caliber. It was available with 5- or 7-inch barrels, and with either blued or nickel-plated finish. These single-action revolvers were not a popular selling item, as the styling was more than twenty years old. The gun was somewhat reminiscent of the earlier Colt Single Action revolver. Remington was to sell only 2,020 Model 1890 revolvers between 1891 and 1894.

THE DENVER GUNMAKERS

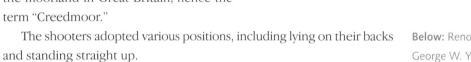

During the 1870s there was a rise in interest in long-range single-shot rifle target shooting in the German schuetzen style. One famous example of schuetzen shooting took place at the Long Range Black Powder match in 1874 at Creedmoor in upstate New York. The competition was between the United States and Ireland and was held at the National Rifle Association's newly established shooting facility which had been built on the site of the Creed farm. The land around this area reminded many of the moorland in Great Britain, hence the term "Creedmoor."

The shooters adopted various positions, including lying on their backs and standing straight up.

To cater for the increasing interest in schuetzen shooting various gunmakers and gun customizers began to produce guns for this style of shooting. These included a group of gunmakers that were based around Denver, Colorado who specialized in fancy modified single-shot rifles.

The Denver gunmakers based much of their output on the successful

Below: Renowned target shooter George W. Yale adopts a laidback shooting style at the Creedmoor range.

Right: Carlos Gove established his gun shop in Denver in 1862. Like many of the other Denver gunsmiths he was a crack shot.

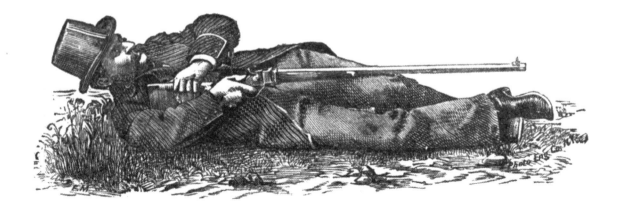

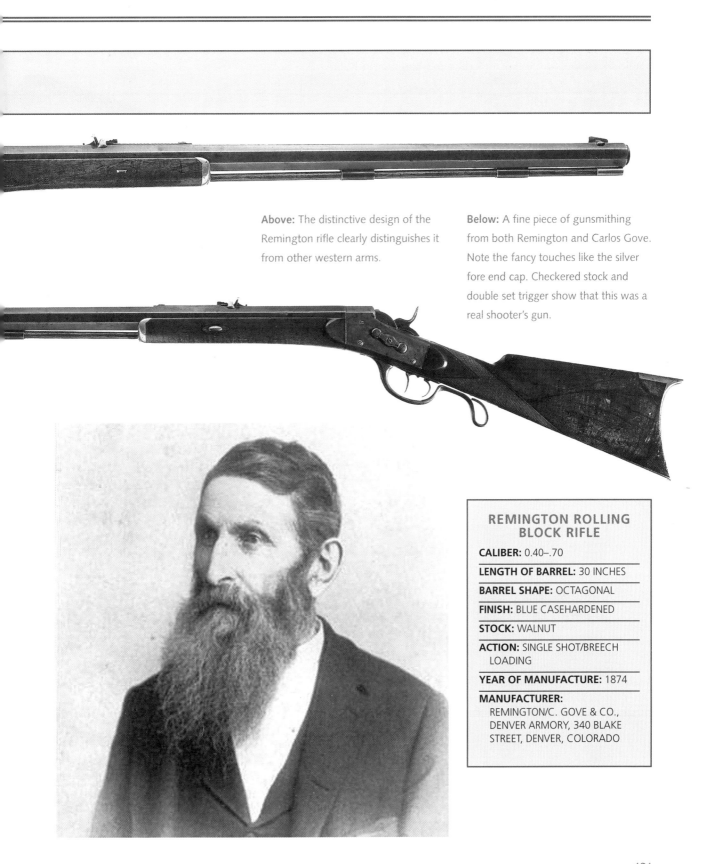

Above: The distinctive design of the Remington rifle clearly distinguishes it from other western arms.

Below: A fine piece of gunsmithing from both Remington and Carlos Gove. Note the fancy touches like the silver fore end cap. Checkered stock and double set trigger show that this was a real shooter's gun.

REMINGTON ROLLING BLOCK RIFLE

CALIBER: 0.40–.70

LENGTH OF BARREL: 30 INCHES

BARREL SHAPE: OCTAGONAL

FINISH: BLUE CASEHARDENED

STOCK: WALNUT

ACTION: SINGLE SHOT/BREECH LOADING

YEAR OF MANUFACTURE: 1874

MANUFACTURER: REMINGTON/C. GOVE & CO., DENVER ARMORY, 340 BLAKE STREET, DENVER, COLORADO

single-shot rifles of the day including the Remington Rolling Block, the Sharps Model 1874, and Winchester's High and Low Wall target-shooting rifles (designed by John Browning).

Gunmakers such as Carlos Gove, J.P. Lower, and George C. Schoyen were part of a thriving western firearms industry that specialized in producing schuetzen type rifles. Some of these gunsmiths had German roots and their skills came from the German tradition.

George Schoyen ran a gun shop in Denver and was one of the premier barrel makers of the time. He was also a very competent target shooter and regularly competed in the area's shooting matches.

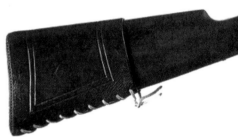

Left: Billy Dixon, United States Army Scout. Dixon was credited as being the greatest shot in the West.

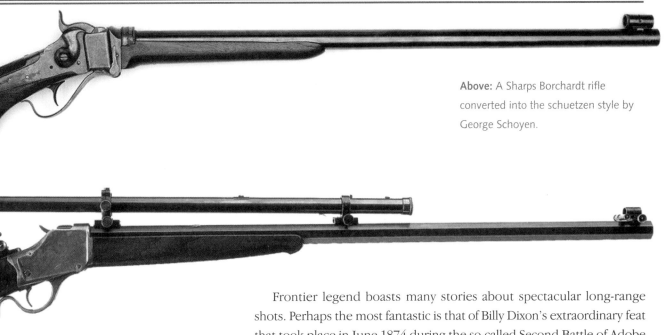

Above: A Sharps Borchardt rifle converted into the schuetzen style by George Schoyen.

Above: George C. Schoyen's personal Winchester Model 1885 that he used to win the Denver Rifle Club Gold Championship Medal in 1895.

Below: A Big Fifty Sharps like the one Billy Dixon used for his amazing feat.

Frontier legend boasts many stories about spectacular long-range shots. Perhaps the most fantastic is that of Billy Dixon's extraordinary feat that took place in June 1874 during the so-called Second Battle of Adobe Walls. This skirmish was fought at the trading post of Adobe Walls, Texas between braves of the Comanche tribe and a group of twenty-eight bison hunters.

William "Billy" Dixon was a scout for the United States Army in the Texas Panhandle and also hunted buffalo for the train companies. But Dixon became famous for his legendary part in the defense of the Adobe Walls settlement armed with his legendary buffalo rifle.

Dixon had led a group of twenty-eight buffalo hunters to Adobe Walls on the Texas Plains as he knew that the area was replete with buffalo. The group was holed up in the outpost when it was attacked by a band of between 700 and 1,200 Comanche warriors on June 27, 1874. The buffalo hunters held the attacking force at bay with their accurate fire for a couple of days. But on the third day Dixon realized that a group of mounted warriors were massing for a raid on the east side of the settlement. He

hastily borrowed a colleague's big fifty Sharps (as he only had a Sharps .45-50) and got off a couple of scratch shots at the insurgents. To Dixon's amazement, his third shot knocked a warrior, who had been sitting right next to Chief Quanah Parker, clean off his horse. Astonishingly, the man had been almost a mile away from Dixon and his shot became known as the "shot of the century." The dispirited attacking force decided to leave the buffalo hunting party alone.

Remington-Walker-Schoyen Hepburn Schuetzen rifle

This is a very fine example of the classic Schuetzen rifle. It is a Remington Walker with a Schoyen barrel. The octagonal barrel is 30 inches long and marked "Geo C. Schoyen, Denver, Colo." The gun has rear vernier sights, a front peep sight, and double set triggers with a ornate schuetzen style scrolled trigger-guard underlever.

REMINGTON-WALKER-SCHOYEN HEPBURN SCHUETZEN RIFLE	
TYPE:	SINGLE–SHOT RIFLE
BARREL LENGTH:	30 INCHES
CALIBER:	.32.40
STOCK:	WALNUT, CHECKERED

Stevens Pope Model 54 Special Order Scoped Single shot rifle

This rifle in the Schuetzen style was made by Stevens Pope with a scope, double set triggers and a checkered walnut inset in the spur lever.

STEVENS POPE MODEL 54	
TYPE:	SINGLE–SHOT RIFLE
BARREL LENGTH:	30 INCHES
CALIBER:	.32-40
STOCK:	WALNUT -CHECKERED

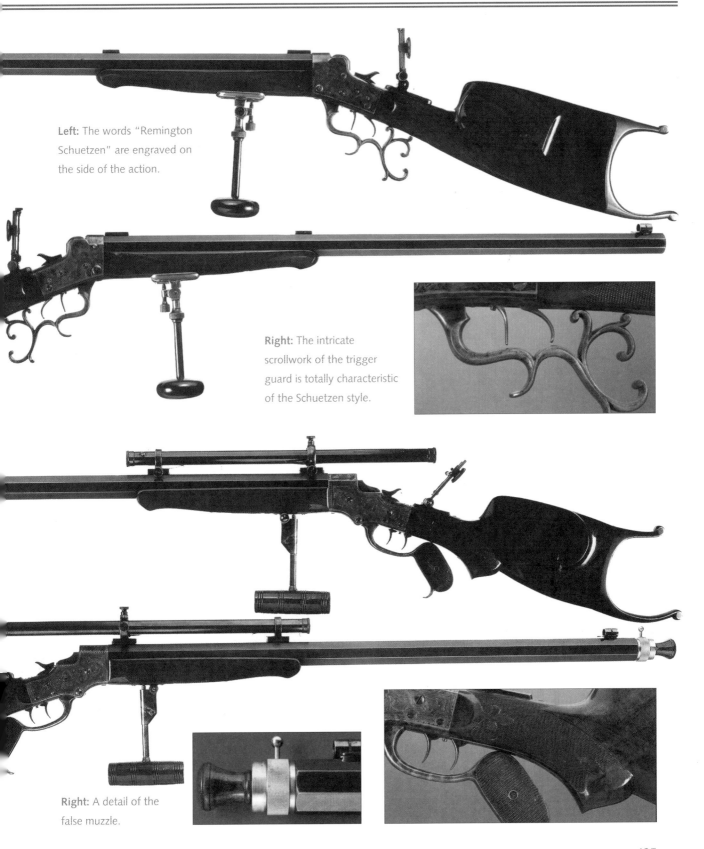

Left: The words "Remington Schuetzen" are engraved on the side of the action.

Right: The intricate scrollwork of the trigger guard is totally characteristic of the Schuetzen style.

Right: A detail of the false muzzle.

SHARPS BORCHRDT SCHUETZEN RIFLE

TYPE: SINGLE–SHOT RIFLE

BARREL LENGTH: 31½ INCHES

CALIBER: .34-40

STOCK: WALNUT WITH FIDDLEBACK FIGURE

Above: A fine Sharps Borchrdt Schuetzen rifle by A.O. Zischang.

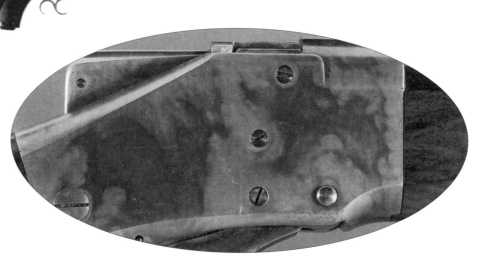

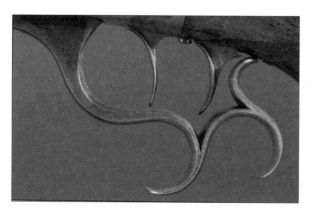

Opposite: George C. Schoyen in his Denver workshop.

GUNFIGHTERS

O f all the wild characters of the western frontier, the gunfighters were perhaps the most feared and flamboyant. They were not simply violent, for in a violent age, this was hardly unique. As the editor of the Kansas City Journal remarked in 1881, "The gentleman who has "killed his man" is by no means a rara avis... He is met daily on Main Street." The gunfighters whose reputations have survived all had some extra characteristic that has kept their image alive: high morals, depravity, good looks, mystery, vicious temper, sadism, marksmanship, or dandyism. In fact the term "gunfighter" did not come into popular use until the 1870s. The earlier term was man-killer, or shootist (as bad man Clay Allison described himself). Gunslingers were an integral part of western life, and existed as a direct result of the conditions there. Whereas the law governed disputes in the East, the gun was the western arbiter of choice. Gunfighters worked on both sides of the law, as both "civilizers" and criminals. Many swapped sides when it suited them. Most were motivated by money, and virtually all were only loyal to their own interests.

Above: A modified Springfield Trapdoor rifle similar to the one that Perry Owens is posing with over the page.

Above: Two views of a Winchester Model 1873 which was one of Commodore Perry Owens chosen weapons.

Commodore Perry Owens

Above: A Colt Peacemaker favored by Perry Owens and many other lawmen and gunfighters.

Commodore Perry Owens was a gunman who stood foursquare on the side of law and order. But his methods were rooted in the gun-slinging style of the Old West, and this soon got him into trouble. Owens ran away from his home at the age of thirteen. Teased for his unusual name, he cultivated a furiously flamboyant appearance, with waist-length strawberry-blonde hair, and a neatly trimmed moustache. He started out as a roping and branding cowboy, but he also worked as a buffalo hunter, and also worked for Wells Fargo. Owens was considered a dead shot, and became famous for his use of the cross-draw of the brace of Colt 1873 pistols he wore slung around his hips. This technique gave him a split-second advantage over his opponents. For tough jobs, he also carried a Winchester 1873, although he also used a modified Springfield trapdoor rifle.

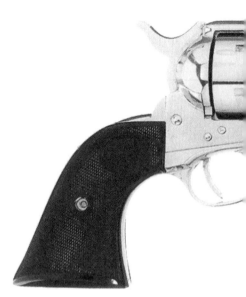

Above: A fine example of the Colt Buntline Special. Legend has it that this was Wyatt Earp's favorite gun.

Left: Commodore Perry Owens was named after the American naval commander, Oliver Hazard Perry.

Wyatt Earp

Wyatt Berry Stapp Earp was another of the West's famous gunslinger lawman who enforced, upheld, and manipulated the law. He grew up on a farm in Illinois, but his family moved west to California in 1864. Wyatt soon found more classic Western employment, taking turns as a shotgun messenger for Wells Fargo, a buffalo hunter, a driver for Phineas Banning's Stage Line, and a railway employee. Later, Earp also mined for copper, gold, and silver and owned several saloons. Earp's weapon of choice was a Colt pistol, either an Army or a Peacemaker. He is also reputed to have carried a Colt Buntline Special, which had a detachable stock. A complex and interesting personality, Earp was considered "a cold fish," and was certainly ruthless, and decisive. Despite this, he was also a loyal friend who formed several lifelong alliances with other famous gunfighters, such as Bat Masterson and Doc Holliday. Like them, he was also a compulsive gambler.

Right: Wyatt Earp, who fought in the most famous shoot-out of all time, at the O.K. Corral.

John Wesley Hardin

Unlike almost all Western gunmen, John Wesley "Wes" Hardin was a professional manslayer by profession. His nicknames and epithets are proof enough of the fear that he inspired. He was variously known as "the meanest man in Texas," "the dark angel of Texas," and as "a homicidal desperado." In common with several other Western bad men, John's father, James G. Hardin, was a preacher. Hardin senior had named his son after the founder of the Methodist faith. Hardin was born on May 26, 1853, in Bonham, Texas. The family did not have a settled home; they were wayfarers who drifted from the home of one relative to another. Despite this, Hardin's parents were highly respected in the various communities in which they lived. But from a very early age it was obvious that John had an extremely violent temper and a vengeful nature. He was almost expelled from his father's own school for attacking another boy, John Sloter, with a knife when he was fourteen. By the age of just fifteen he had made his first kill. His victim was a black ex-slave known as Mage. In later life, Hardin attempted to justify his flight from justice by saying that "To be tried at that time for the killing of a Negro meant certain death at the hands of a court backed by Northern bayonets."

After a bloody career in which he claimed to have killed at least forty men, Hardin moved to El Paso in 1895. Here he became a lawyer and settled down to write his autobiography. But Hardin couldn't leave his violent past behind and soon became involved in a cocktail of gambling and gun crime. Consequentially, he was shot down in El Paso's Acme Saloon at the age of forty-two. When he died, Hardin was carrying a 38 caliber, $2^1/_2$-inch barrel Colt Model 1877 Lightning revolver with mother-of-pearl grips (serial number 84304). The gun had been presented to him by a grateful client and was shipped to him from the Colt factory in 1891. Unfortunately for him, Wes Hardin never got a chance to draw this elegant firearm from its tooled leather holster that he had bought in El Paso. His previous gun had also been a Colt revolver: an 1877 .41 caliber Thunderer. Hardin had used this gun to hold up and rob the Gem Saloon.

COLT MODEL 1877 DOUBLE-ACTION "LIGHTNING" AND "THUNDERER"

TYPE: CENTERFIRE, DOUBLE-ACTION REVOLVER

ORIGIN: COLT PFA MFG CO., HARTFORD, CONNECTICUT

CALIBER: LIGHTNING .38 COLT; THUNDERER .41 COLT

BARREL LENGTH: SEE TEXT

Above: A Colt Lightning with a 4½-inch barrel in a worn blued finish. This model has a ejector rod for reloading.

Above: A Colt Lightning with a bright nickel finish and a 3½-inch barrel.

Above: The Colt Lightning with the shortest barrel option of 2½-inches. Both of the shorter barreled guns had to be reloaded by unscrewing the knurled spindle under the barrel.

Right: This Model Lightning has a 4½-inch barrel. It was made for American Express.

Above & below: This is the .41 caliber Thunderer and is shown in two barrel lengths of 3½- and 4½-inches. John Wesley Hardin is known to have carried this type of gun.

COLT LIGHTNING 41

Opposite: John Wesley Hardin in a studio photograph

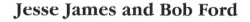

Jesse James and Bob Ford

Robert or "Bob" Ford has the unenviable distinction among Western gunfighters of being defined for posterity by the man he murdered: the far more celebrated Jesse James.

Celebrated as "the dirty little coward," Robert Newton Ford was born in 1861 in Ray County, Missouri. From childhood, Robert hero-worshipped Jesse James, and read the nickel novels his hero inspired. Bob finally got to meet James in 1880. He

Above: A studio shot of Jesse James taken just before his death in 1882.

Left: Bob Ford pictured in about 1880 with a Colt Single-Action revolver.

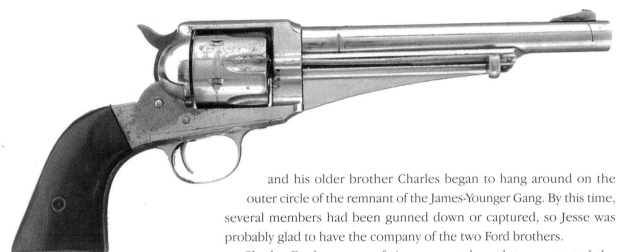

Above: A Remington Model 1875 similar to the gun carried by gang member Frank James. This example has the later blade sight.

and his older brother Charles began to hang around on the outer circle of the remnant of the James-Younger Gang. By this time, several members had been gunned down or captured, so Jesse was probably glad to have the company of the two Ford brothers.

Charles Ford was one of six gang members that perpetrated the James-Younger Gang's final train robbery at Blue Cut, where they absconded with around $3,000 in cash and jewelry from the passengers. Robert did not take part in any specific crimes, but was happy to mind the gang's horses and be ready to help. Jesse invited the Ford brothers to join him in what was to be his final crime. James planned to raid the Platte City Bank and set himself up as a gentleman farmer.

But events began to take a terrible turn in January 1882 when two wanted James Gang members took refuge in the farmhouse home of the Ford brothers' sister, Martha Bolton. This pair of bandits, Wood Hite

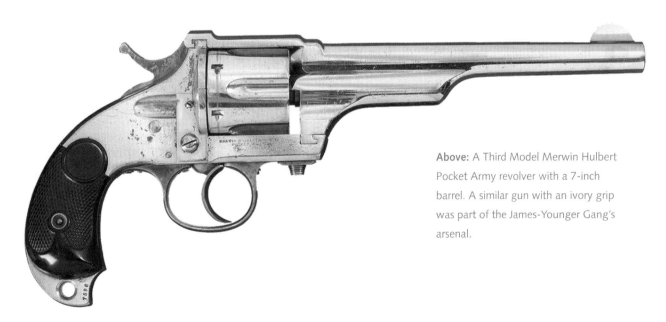

Above: A Third Model Merwin Hulbert Pocket Army revolver with a 7-inch barrel. A similar gun with an ivory grip was part of the James-Younger Gang's arsenal.

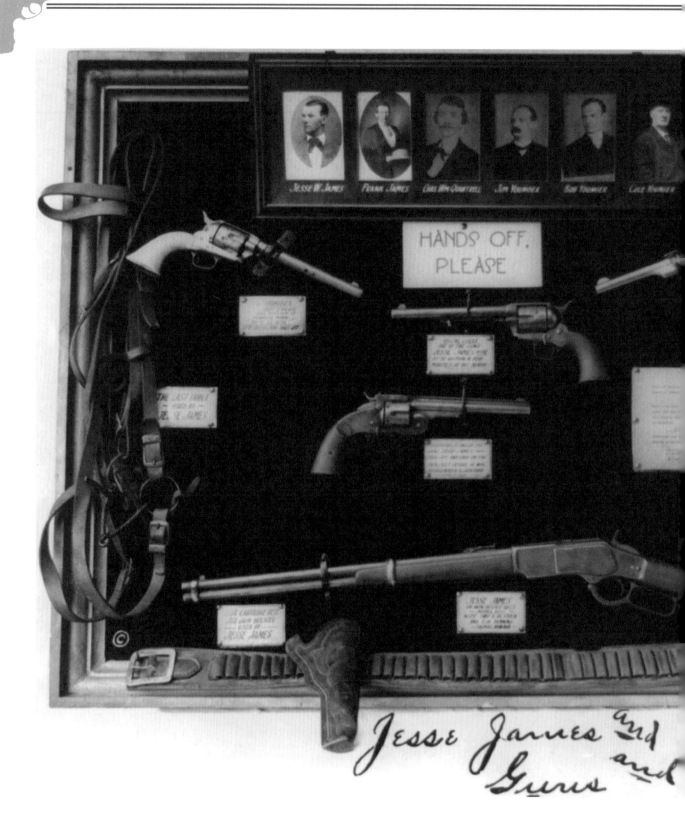

and Dick Liddil, fell into a quarrel about Martha's favors and drew their weapons. Robert Ford was friendly with Liddil and promptly shot Hite (a cousin of the James brothers) in the head. Missouri's newly elected Governor, Thomas T. Crittenden, brought in Bob Ford to answer for the murder. Fearful of being hanged and mindful that the governor had offered a huge reward for the capture of Jesse James, Ford told Kansas City police commissioner Henry Craig that he could deliver the outlaw to him, alive or dead. Craig was sick of the James brothers' criminality and was determined to eradicate them. On January 13, 1882, Ford cut a deal with the governor for a pardon for the murder of Wood Hite and the reward of $10,000 to capture or assassinate Jesse James. No doubt he also hoped to make a name for himself as the man who brought Jesse James to justice.

In the spring of that year Jesse James was living in the small town of St Joseph, Missouri, using the false identity of J.D. Howard. Bob Ford and his brother Charlie visited Jesse on April 3, 1882. As the men discussed the upcoming raid on the Platte City Bank, Jesse uncharacteristically put down his gun belt and stood on a chair with his back to the Ford brothers. Legend had it that he went to adjust a framed needlepoint on the wall which was hanging crooked. As he did so, Bob Ford drew a Smith & Wesson Model 3, a single-action top-break revolver, and shot James in the back of the head.

It was at this point that everything started to go horribly wrong for the Ford brothers. Despite the deal that Bob Ford had cut with the governor, they were immediately arrested, tried, and sentenced for James's murder. They were then pardoned by Governor Crittenden. Thoroughly shaken, the brothers were grateful to be given just a small portion of the massive reward they had been promised.

The Ford brothers' subsequent life became completely nightmarish. Forced to earn a living by acting out nightly their betrayal of Jesse James in a touring stage show, they both felt the strain. Charles Ford fell ill with tuberculosis and became addicted to morphine. Worn down by remorse and self-loathing, he committed suicide on May 4, 1884. Bob Ford was reduced to posing for photographs as the "man who killed Jesse James" in dime museums. Later in 1884, Ford and Dick Liddil opened a saloon in Las Vegas, New Mexico, but Ford was forced to leave

Left: A collection of equipment owned by Jesse James and his gang, the Outlaws.

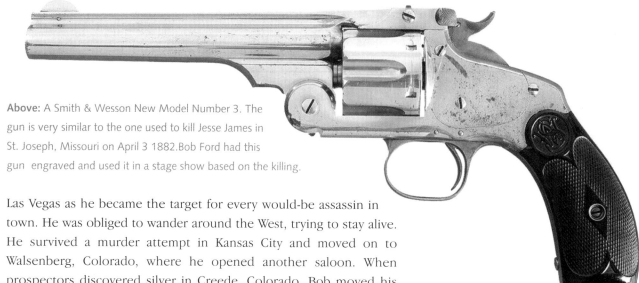

Above: A Smith & Wesson New Model Number 3. The gun is very similar to the one used to kill Jesse James in St. Joseph, Missouri on April 3 1882. Bob Ford had this gun engraved and used it in a stage show based on the killing.

Las Vegas as he became the target for every would-be assassin in town. He was obliged to wander around the West, trying to stay alive. He survived a murder attempt in Kansas City and moved on to Walsenberg, Colorado, where he opened another saloon. When prospectors discovered silver in Creede, Colorado, Bob moved his business there. He opened Ford's Exchange saloon on May 29, 1892. Six days later it was burned to the ground (supposedly by the Soapy Smith Gang). The resilient Ford opened a tent saloon in the town until he could rebuild. But just three days later, on June 8, 1892 Edward Capehart O'Kelley strolled into his business with a sawn-off shotgun. "Hello, Bob," he called out to Ford, who turned around to see who it was. Kelley discharged both barrels into Ford, killing him instantly. O'Kelley himself became notorious as the "man who killed the man who killed Jesse James." It has been alleged that the notorious conman Soapy Smith had convinced O'Kelley that he would become a popular hero for killing the unpopular Ford.

The Rose of Cimarron

Western men didn't have the monopoly on being outlaws. The Rose of Cimarron, AKA Rose Dunn, came from humble roots in Oklahoma

REMINGTON DOUBLE BARREL MODEL 1889 SHOTGUN	
CALIBER: 12 GAUGE	
LENGTH OF BARREL: 18 INCHES	
BARREL SHAPE: ROUND	
FINISH: BROWNED STEEL	
GRIPS: WALNUT, CHECKERED WITH PISTOL GRIP	
ACTION: BREECH LOADING DOUBLE BARREL	
YEAR OF MANUFACTURE: 1889	
MANUFACTURER: REMINGTON ARMS COMPANY, ILION, NEW YORK	

Above: Bob Ford was blasted to death by a sawn-off shotgun.

Territory. Her family was poor, but she was well educated at a convent in Wichita, Kansas. She met Doolin Gang member George "Bittercreek" Newcomb through her two older brothers who were themselves minor outlaws. Rose was infatuated by Newcomb despite the fact that she was just fifteen years old. She became a valued member of the Doolin gang, helping them by buying supplies and nursing them when they got wounded in the course of their criminal activities. In September 1893 a posse of United States marshals pinned down the gang in Ingalls, Oklahoma. An almighty shootout ensued in which Newcomb was injured. While her lover lay wounded in the street, Rose fetched ammunition and a Winchester rifle. The story goes that she helped him to escape by giving him covering fire while he reloaded his revolvers and fled the scene. Three marshals were killed during the gunfight and Newcomb and Charlie Pierce (another Doolin gang member) were wounded. Rose spent two months in hiding with the gang nursing Newcomb and Pierce back to health. In the meantime Rose's brothers had become bounty hunters, calling themselves The Dunn Brothers.

Because Newcomb had a bounty of $5,000 on his head, dead or alive, he became an interesting target for the Dunn Brothers in their new career. The fact that he was their sister's lover apparently made no difference to them. As the unsuspecting Newcomb, still on the run from the United States marshals, arrived at the Dunn home with fellow outlaw Charley Pierce to visit Rose in May 1895, the Dunn brothers gunned down Newcomb and Pierce in cold blood.

Rose herself was never prosecuted for her involvement with the gang. But her brief but active outlaw life gave her a great deal of notoriety and she became a western legend. She eventually joined polite society by marrying a local politician, and lived the remainder of her life on the right side of the law. It is thought she died in 1953, at the age of seventy-three.

Below: Rose Dunn, AKA The Rose of Cimarron, is pictured with her Colt Model 1878 in .45 caliber.

COLT MODEL 1878 FRONTIER

The Colt Model 1878 appeared shortly after the Model 1877 and was another double-action revolver but larger and more robust, with a strong frame and a removable trigger guard. The fluted cylinder held six cartridges and was not removable, being loaded via narrow gate on the right side of the frame. There were six barrel lengths (3, 3.5, 4, 4.75, 5.5, and 7.5 inches) and a wide variety of chambering from .22 to .476. A total of some 51,000 was produced in 1878 through 1905, which included some 4,000 Model 1878/1902, ordered by the US Army in 1902 for use in Alaska and the Philippines.

Above: The Frontier was widely used in the American West and this example, one of a series known as the Sheriff's Model, was used by Sheriff J.H. Ward of Vinta County, as shown by the engraving on the backstrap. His revolver was .44-40 caliber and had a 4.1/2-inch barrel.

COLT MODEL 1878 FRONTIER	
CALIBER:	0.44-40
LENGTH OF BARREL:	4 INCHES
BARREL SHAPE:	ROUND
FINISH:	BLUE/GRAY MIXED WITH SURFACE RUST
GRIPS:	HARD RUBBER
ACTION:	DOUBLE
YEAR OF MANUFACTURE:	1878
MANUFACTURER:	COLT

WESTERN GAMBLERS

Among the many types of men and women who came west to exploit other westerners, the gamblers were some of the most colorful. Gambling reflected the very character of the region, with its willingness to take chances, and its spirit of adventure. Almost every Western movie shows men, and occasionally women, playing cards, roulette, or other games of chance. Gambling and liquor were the twin attractions of the thousands of saloons that spring up in the region, and gaming became an integral part of frontier life.

As the rest of America became less tolerant of gambling and other forms of vice, many professional gamblers made a strategic move to the West. Their first targets were the Mississippi riverboats, and it is estimated that between 600 and 800 "gamesmen" worked the boats in the 1840s.

Famous gamblers like Charles Cora made huge fortunes on the river. Notorious as the Mississippi's foremost faro player, Cora was reputed to have won over $85,000 in six months. Riverboat gamblers Jimmy Fitzgerald and Charles Starr were equally renowned for their sartorial elegance. The originators of the riverboat gamblers' sharp dress code, the pair was always attired in the epitome of good style. They sported expensive black suits and boots, ruffled white shirts, brocaded vests, conspicuous jewelry, and silver-topped walking canes. As gambling moved westwards the professional gamblers moved with it and soon every western town had a gambling establishment in its saloon.

Opposite: Gambling was a very popular pastime for men on the frontier but it attracted crime and violence.

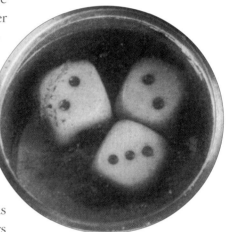

Above: The ivory top of a gambler's cane contains three dice in a silver-plated canister.

Below: Highly ornate poker chips from the days of the frontier.

Deringers and Vest Guns

As the West progressed, a new breed of men arrived. Clad in tailored jackets and dust-free Derby hats, the gamblers had hit town. Unlike the cowboys, these men did not wear large Colts holstered in plain view, preferring to hide small but deadly, short-barreled guns about their person. These were often concealed in a vest pocket, inside a hatband, or in a well-tailored sleeve. Guns like these settled many an accusation of cheating. Guns like these were also popular with saloon girls and more respectable ladies. They were ideal for self-defense and could be concealed in a purse or a garter. Here is a selection of these weapons of concealment.

1 Tipping & Lawden 4-barrel pistol
Four barrels are better than one. Master Gunsmiths Tipping & Lawden of Birmingham, England manufactured this Sharps design. It was then imported into The United States. The gun has 3-inch barrels and is .31 caliber. It is lavishly decorated with much engraving and pearl grips.

2 ,3, 4 Colt Deringers
These are three examples of the Colt Third Model Deringer. The gun was designed by Alexander Thuer, and was often known as the "Thuer Derringer." All three examples are .41 caliber weapons with 2½-inch barrels. The barrels pivoted to one side for loading.

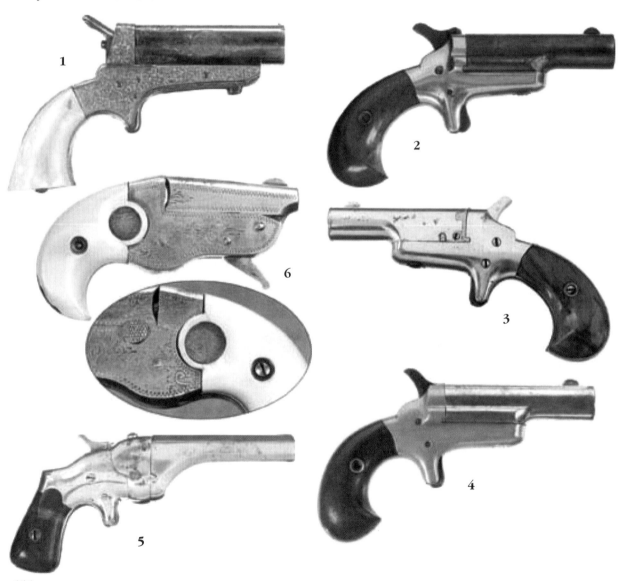

5 Hammond Bulldog

This is a crudely finished single-shot selfdefense weapon of .44 caliber. Nevertheless, it would be effective at close range. It has a 4-inch barrel and must have kicked like a mule!

6 Hopkins & Allen Vest Pocket Deringer

This cleverly camouflaged trinket was just 1¾ inches long, and fired a .22 caliber round. It could (literally) fit in the palm of the shooter's hand, and be concealed until the last moment.

7 National No2 Deringer

Moore's Patent Firearm Company was established in Brooklyn in the mid-nineteenth century. The company changed its name to The National Arms Company in 1866. This gun is the No. 2 Model. It has a spur trigger, and is loaded by dropping the barrel down to one side. Following the takeover of the company by Colt in 1870, this design was marketed as the Colt No. 2 Deringer.

8 Remington Elliot Ring Trigger Pistol

This pistol relied on four solid static barrels to deliver four shots. It was chambered for .32 caliber ammunition. The ring trigger was pushed forward to rotate the firing pin, then pulled back to cock the mechanism and fire.
9 Remington No2 Vest Pocket Pistol
Designed by Joseph Rider, this .32 caliber vest pocket pistol fired a single shot. It was equipped with the unique Rider split-breech loading system, and had a 3¼-inch barrel.

10 Remington Double Deringer

This was the ultimate design for last ditch defense. The over-and-under barrel layout was less cumbersome and heavy than that of multi-barrel guns. The gun was also reliable, and fired two rounds in .41 caliber: an assailant-stopping load. The gun became extremely popular and over 150,000 were manufactured between 1866 and 1935.

11 Sharps pepperbox

Strictly speaking, this design by master gunsmith Christian Sharps is a multi-barreled pistol rather than a pepperbox. Nonetheless, the gun became a very popular weapon. The gun was reloaded by sliding the barrel block forward along a rail to access the breech. The four-barrel system was static and the firing pin rotated to fire each chamber in turn.

12 Wheeler Double Deringer

This weapon was designed and manufactured by the American Arms Company. It features two vertically-mounted barrels that were rotated manually. This example has a 3-inch barrel block, chambered for two .32 caliber rounds. It has a nickel-plated frame, a spur trigger, and blued barrels.

WELLS FARGO

Above: Wells Fargo issued all their operatives with recognizable badges and their logo became a symbol of civilization moving westwards.

Wells Fargo was one of the great institutions of the West and was a positive force for the civilizing of the Wild Frontier. Its very name conjures a thrilling image of a six-horse stagecoach loaded with gold, thundering across the romantic plains landscape. The Wells Fargo business became part of the fabric of the American West. The company served people of every background and profession and actively sought to control lawlessness. The company's first office was established in downtown San Francisco at 420 Montgomery Street, right in the heart of the tent city of the '49ers.

The new company offered banking (buying gold, selling bank drafts) and express, secure carriage for all kinds of cargo, especially gold dust and gold bullion from the newly sunk mines. Right from the beginning, there was also a thread of altruism and equality in the company's culture. Wells Fargo offered their services to "all men, women, or children, rich or poor, white or black." They ran their business for all the settlers and the frontier people of the West, including blacks, whites, and Spanish-speaking Hispanics.

Integrity was a great factor in the success of the business. Wells Fargo agents often became trusted figures in the new towns and volatile mining settlements of the West.

Agents were recruited from well-respected members of the community, including storekeepers and attorneys, and each agent was given a certificate of appointment by Wells Fargo. As well as the Express service, the agents also offered basic banking and financial services.

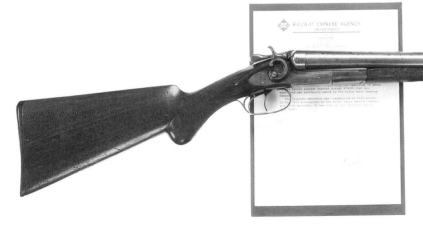

Above: Documented Wells Fargo Hammer shotgun.

Left: The Wells Fargo stagecoaches were often subject to hold-ups, from desperados attracted by the gold and valuables they often conveyed. Armed guards usually protected these shipments.

Below: A Wells Fargo inscription above the barrels of the Wells Fargo Remington shotgun featured on the facing page.

The company started their overland stagecoach line in the 1860s and also took over the Butterfield Overland Mail Company which had been established in 1858. Wells Fargo sent the mail by the fastest means possible: stagecoach, steamship, railroad, pony rider, or telegraph. Their operatives often brought the mail through at dreadful personal risk. Wells Fargo also employed detectives

to investigate fraud and any other illegal practices in connection with their business, and also engaged armed escorts and shotgun riders to discourage theft and hold-ups. The guards were reputed to carry cut down shotguns, which were easy to conceal under the seat of a wagon and lethal at close quarters. This modus operandi daunted many would-be villains.

Opposite: Wells Fargo guard Madison Larkin photographed with his shotgun and sidearm in Phoenix, Arizona in 1877.

WESTERN SHOTGUNS

The shotgun is ideal for close-range defense and offense, and was used by lawmen and outlaws alike. Shotguns are usually loaded with lead pellets or buckshot and are fired from the hip. This results in terrible devastation at short range, without the need for taking careful aim. They were used by Wells Fargo guards, sheriffs, and bank robbers as well as homesteaders and ranchers.

Parker Shotgun

Charles Parker's sons took over his company in 1868. They recognized the peacetime need for shotguns, and designed this classic side-by-side shotgun with external hammers. Many owners had the barrels of their Parker shotgun shortened.

Winchester Model 1887 Lever Action Shotgun

This Browning-designed gun was sold with either a 30- or 32-inch barrel, in either 10- or 12-gauge. The five-shot magazine was housed in a tube under the barrel. A Riot version was also available, with a 20-inch barrel. The Model was a favorite with the Texas Rangers.

THE WESTERN STOREKEEPER

Almost every frontier town had a general store, which was a focal point for the community. The store was a meeting point for townsfolk where they could exchange gossip or shelter from the cold and warm themselves around the stove. But stores also became targets for thieves and robbers. Most storekeepers were sedentary types from back East and were no physical match for the rough and tough

cowhands and hard bitten trail bums that were likely to come looking for free merchandise. This situation brings Colt's famous adage to mind, "God made man but Colonel Colt made them equal." Taking this maxim to heart, most storekeepers kept a firearm under the shop counter.

Colt realised that this was a great market opportunity and devised a

Below: An interesting lineup of stores, catering for life's necessities – liquor, cigars, dry goods, and clothing.

short-barrelled revolver known as the Colt 1882 Sheriff's (or Storekeeper's) revolver. This gun was a derivative of the 1873 single-action model. The sheriff's revolver is minus the ejector rod of its counterpart. Colt produced variants of the gun between 1882 and 1898 with several different calibres. Around 70,000 units were made. For a compact weapon the gun packed a considerable punch, using the full-size model's 45 caliber center-fire ammunition. Shortened handguns like this one were convenient for concealment and quick to draw, which made them useful for both defensive and offensive firing.

Opposite: A re-creation of a typical general store. Its wonderful interior is stocked with everything a frontiersperson could need – besom brooms, oven paddles, salt pork (in the barrels), dried meat, grain, flour, molasses, oil lamps, pitchers, pans, and dainty china.

COLT 1882 STORE-KEEPER'S REVOLVER

CALIBER:	0.44-40
LENGTH OF BARREL:	3-INCH
CARTRIDGE CAPACITY:	SIX-SHOT
FIRING SYSTEM:	CENTER-FIRE
GRIP:	BLACK RUBBER
OPERATION:	SINGLE-ACTION
WEIGHT:	33 1/3 OUNCES
OVERALL LENGTH:	8½ INCHES
SAFETY:	HALF-COCK HAMMER
MANUFACTURER:	COLT

A HISTORY OF BROWNING FIREARMS

John Moses Browning (1855–1926) is widely acknowledged to be one of the greatest firearms designers of all time. Indeed, many people would insist that he was the greatest. John's father, Jonathan Browning (1805-1879) was also a gunsmith and designed several unusual rifles, but was simply not in the same extraordinary league as his son. John Browning's creative output included 128 patents and at least eighty separate designs.

John and his brothers lived in the tiny frontier town of Ogden, Utah. This was typical "Old West" country, linked to the eastern states by a series of long and tenuous roads and trails, until the railroad came to the area in 1869.

Despite such relative isolation and having left school at the age of

fifteen after a typical rural education, John was to become a highly respected businessman and inventor. He first worked on a national scale, collaborating with the well-established armories of Colt, Remington, Stevens, and Winchester. Later, he became internationally renowned. He travelled regularly to Europe to visit his closest business partner Fabrique Nationale d'Armes de Guerre which was established in 1889 in Liege, Belgium. Browning also became closely involved with the United States government and with the United States Army and Navy, whose officers treated him with the greatest respect.

Browning's designs covered the whole range of small arms, from semi-automatic pistols to single-shot rifles. He also developed many different types of repeater rifles and machine guns. His brain was constantly active and he conducted a never-ending search for firearms perfection. One of Browning's greatest assets was that he was a highly enthusiastic shot and practiced his skills on ranges and in competitions and also in the hills, fields, and forests around Ogden. Here, he was able to loose off thousands of rounds from each weapon, detecting and analysing shortcomings and devising remedies which could then be implemented in his workshop.

In writing about the Browning story, it is important to stress that his Ogden workshop was not a firearms production facility. The shop sold and repaired hardware, including farming implements and tools. Browning's firearms business was confined to making and refining his designs, and to selling and repairing firearms which had been produced elsewhere. Apart from weapons designed by the father, Jonathan Browning, and the first 600 examples of John Brownings's single-shot rifle, only prototypes of his designs were made there. When John sold his designs to other companies, he also gave up the right to manufacture them.

John Browning's designs were made under license by both American and foreign firearms companies, but many "clones" of Browning weapons have also been produced. These are exact copies of Browning weapons but all too often these have been manufactured to far less rigorous engineering standards.

Opposite: The famous Four Bs: G.L. Becker, John M. Browning, A.P. Bigelow, and Matthew S. Browning. They formed Utah's premier live-bird shooting team. Like many successful gunsmiths, Browning was interested in shooting and was a crackshot.

Following pages: John M. Browning's workbench at his gun shop in Ogden, Utah.

Browning and Winchester

As time went on, Browning's hometown of Ogden expanded rapidly. This was mainly because of its status as a railroad junction. The ease of travel and communication that the railroad brought with it was of inestimable value to the Browning brothers' business, which was now in direct railroad contact with the eastern states. In 1882 John Browning took out two more firearms patents. The reputation of the Browning single-shot rifle was spreading and production proceeded steadily in Ogden. In 1883 Browning had one of those lucky breaks which all inventors need, when one of the Winchester Repeating Arms Company's salesmen happened to try one of Browning's single-shot rifles. Immediately recognizing its merits, the salesman bought the gun for $15 and sent it to the Winchester factory for examination. Winchester had a serious gap in its product line for just such a single-shot rifle and the company's management board took less than a week to decide to acquire Browning's design. Accordingly, they dispatched the general manager, T.G. Bennett, to discover as much as possible about Browning's business, as it was unknown in the East. That the general manager of one of the world's greatest firearms companies should personally undertake such a journey is an extraordinary compliment to both John Browning and the quality of his designs. Bennett arrived unannounced and found the young brothers busy at their lathes and anvils. His discussion with Browning was short, sharp, and to the point, and ended with Bennett writing a letter of understanding on the shop counter.

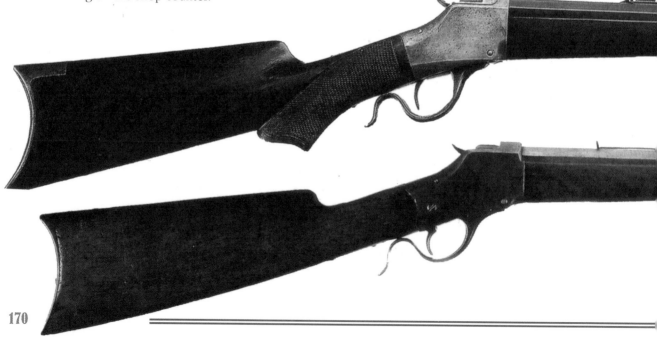

This first contract between John Browning and the Winchester Repeating Arms Company granted the latter the sole manufacturing and sales rights for the price of $8,000. This made the Browning brothers fairly rich by the general standard of the times and fantastically rich by local Utah standards. In today's terms the contract would be worth between one half and one million dollars, depending on the conversion factor used. By any standard this was a huge amount of money for a tiny company based in the remote town of Ogden.

But Winchester was delighted with their purchase. The gun was a godsend to the company and they began to manufacture the gun as quickly as possible. It was launched onto the market in 1885. Browning's design was so inherently robust, reliable, and adaptable that it could be adjusted to use a wide range of cartridges from the .50 Winchester Express down to the .22 Short.

A minor problem arose when Bennett discovered that, in all innocence, the brothers were continuing to produce single-shot rifles in their own workshop to meet existing orders and he courteously explained that they had transferred all production rights in the model to Winchester. As with all their contracts with Browning, Winchester's policy was to purchase exclusive rights to patents outright; the company never agreed to pay royalties. At first glance, this policy may appear one-sided, but it also had some advantages for John Browning. On many occasions Winchester purchased patents of firearms that they knew they would never put into production for one reason or another. This meant

Below: An extremely rare Browning Semi-Deluxe single-shot rifle. This design was purchased by Winchester and mass-produced as the Model 1885.

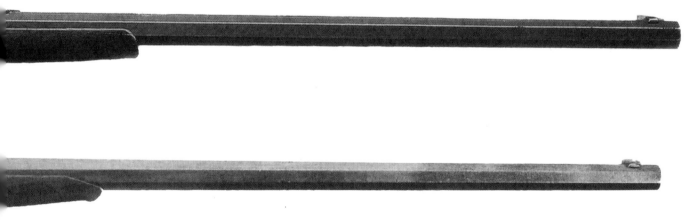

Below: An early production Winchester Model 1885 High Wall rifle. This very closely resembled the Browning prototype.

that Browning was the only person to make any money from these designs.

When he came up with his next design for a lever-action rifle, John Browning decided that he would take the prototype to Winchester himself. Previous to making this journey, the furthest that Browning and his brother Matt had travelled was the thirty-five miles to Salt Lake City. The brothers travelled by transcontinental train to New York City and, after a night seeing the sights in the big city, they went on to New Haven, Connecticut. Even by rail, the journey took six days. Winchester took one look at Browning's lever-action rifle and realized that it was way ahead of any other rifle in the world. They bought it immediately, reputedly paying Browning a one-off lump sum of $50,000.

Having bought the production rights for five Browning guns, Winchester commissioned Browning to design a specific weapon

Left: The Browning gun store in Ogden, Utah.

Opposite: John M. Browning with the rifle that became both the Remington Model 24 and the Browning .22 Automatic. The characteristic loading port of the buttstock is clearly visible.

especially for them. They wanted a lever-action, repeating shotgun. Browning agreed that such a weapon was possible but said that he would prefer to produce a slide-action weapon. Nevertheless, Browning delivered the prototype of the gun Winchester had ordered in June 1885. Winchester was delighted with his design. They immediately tooled up to produce the gun and entered it in their catalog as the Winchester Model 1887. In just three years, John Browning had produced three outstanding designs for Winchester, the Models 1885, 1886, and 1887.

Sometimes Browning produced a new design by himself but he also responded to suggestions from Winchester. The Winchester Model 92, for example, was the result of a request from Bennett for an entirely new design built around the .40-40 cartridge. The gun was to replace the Model 73. During one of John's visits to New Haven, Bennett offered him $10,000 if a prototype of the 92 could be ready in three months' time. John delivered it at New Haven within just one month. This included both his trip back to Ogden and the time it took the rifle to arrive in Connecticut. Browning was paid $20,000 for his efforts, but the gun proved to be a tremendous bargain for Winchester who went on to sell a million units.

John Moses Browning collapsed and died in his office at the Fabrique Nationale factory in Liege, Belgium, in 1926. He was surrounded by many of his family and by the workers whom he respected, in a factory whose fortunes he had done so much to secure. It was a fitting end to the life of a truly great man.

Browning's amazing story closes the chronicle of the traditional guns and gunmakers of the nineteenth century. The fact that Browning had

Above: A fancy engraved version of the Winchester Model 1892 that used Browning's Model 1886 action. This example is a takedown sporting rifle with a 20-inch barrel chambered for .25-20 ammunition.

already invented the automatic pistol by the turn of that century poses
an intriguing question. What if the age of the western gunfighter had
crossed with this extraordinary weapon? Imagine the gunfight at the
O.K. Corral if the shooters had been armed with Colt Model 1900s or
the James Gang had toted automatics! And yet just a few short years
separate these events.

Winchester Model 1890

The Model 1890, designed by the brothers John and Matthew Browning,
was Winchester's first-ever slide-action rifle and achieved world-wide
popularity, with a total of 775,000 produced between 1890 and 1932. All
Model 1890s had 24-inch barrels and were available in either .22 Short,
.22 Long, or .22 WRF chamberings, with .22 LR being added in 1919 (the
.22 WRF was developed specially for the Model 1890).

WINCHESTER MODEL 1890	
TYPE:	SLIDE-ACTION RIFLE
ORIGIN:	WINCHESTER REPEATING ARMS COMPANY, NEW HAVEN, CONNECTICUT
CALIBER:	.22 (SEE TEXT)
BARREL:	24IN

Winchester Model 1895 lever-action rifle

A very early production Model 1895 with the flat-sided receiver, which
characterizes the first 5,000 (actual serial of this weapon is #3797). It
has a 28-inch .30–30 caliber barrel and clearly shows the unmistakable
profile created by the integral magazine.

WINCHESTER MODEL 1895 LEVER-ACTION RIFLE	
TYPE:	LEVER-ACTION, BOX MAGAZINE-FED RIFLE
ORIGIN:	WINCHESTER REPEATING ARMS COMPANY, NEW HAVEN, CONNECTICUT
CALIBER:	SEE TEXT
BARREL:	SEE TEXT

ACKNOWLEDGEMENTS

Patrick F Hogan, Rock Island Auction Co.

The National Archives

Colorado History Society

Kathy Weiser, Legends of America

Kansas State Historical Society

Patrick Reardon, Civil War Collection

Don Troiani, Civil War paintings

Ken Crosby, alias "Bronco," for access to his collection of weapons